I0017255

SCRATCH PROGRAMMING

A Complete Step-by-Step Guide for Beginners in Understanding Power Bi

Mike Morris

© Copyright 2019 Mike Morris - All rights reserved.

This document is geared towards providing exact and reliable information in regards to the topic and issue covered. The publication is sold with the idea that the publisher is not required to render accounting, officially permitted, or otherwise, qualified services. If advice is necessary, legal or professional, a practiced individual in the profession should be ordered.

- From a Declaration of Principles which was accepted and approved equally by a Committee of the American Bar Association and a Committee of Publishers and Associations.

In no way is it legal to reproduce, duplicate, or transmit any part of this document in either electronic means or in printed format. Recording of this publication is strictly prohibited and any storage of this document is not allowed unless with written permission from the publisher. All rights reserved.

The information provided herein is stated to be truthful and consistent, in that any liability, in terms of inattention or otherwise, by any usage or abuse of any policies, processes, or directions contained within is the solitary and utter responsibility of the recipient reader. Under no circumstances will any legal responsibility or blame be held against the publisher for any reparation, damages, or monetary loss due to the information herein, either directly or indirectly.

Respective authors own all copyrights not held by the publisher.

The information herein is offered for informational purposes solely, and is universal as so. The presentation of the information is without contract or any type of guarantee assurance.

The trademarks that are used are without any consent, and the publication of the trademark is without permission or backing by the trademark owner. All trademarks and brands within this book are for clarifying purposes only and are the owned by the owners themselves, not affiliated with this document.

Table of Contents

Introduction

Scratch is a programming language that is suitable for people of all ages. It gives an entertaining and rich environment in which you can learn through different interactive projects. By using Scratch a person can easily learn how to make media-rich content such as games, animations, reports, etc. Scratch is designed to enable you to access options that you couldn't use if you weren't a professional programmer. This user-friendly programming language has a wide range of tools (especially multimedia ones), so you can make many different applications. And the best thing is that with Scratch it is way easier since it is simpler to use. We can say that Scratch is a booster for developing your problem-solving skills too, and not only for programming but for many other aspects of life.

The environment in Scratch has the advantage of quick feedback so it is very easy to check if your solution is correct. This way of working allows you to try different paths and improves your logic during doing things. Since this programming language is very visual and its structure is based on having a large amount of multimedia content, it is not hard to trace the flow of your project. The main idea of Scratch is to make computer science and its ideas accessible to a larger number of people.

Scratch is made to motivate you to learn through discovery and exploration. It requires imagination and creativity, which makes it approachable, even to those who are absolute beginners. There are a lot of guides and books that can help you with Scratch. However, these books usually target younger people and they mostly offer just a few simple application examples so you can understand the user interface in Scratch. Keep in mind that most of those books are talking about Scratch more than about the programming in it. That is why in this guide we will try to explain the basics of programming and its fundamental concepts while using Scratch as a tool for better understanding.

This means that this guide is for all those who want to learn more about computer sciences. It covers the most important concepts in programming whether you use it for school assignments or just as a self-learning guide. We will cover basic programming skills and knowledge using the language that is understandable to the people regardless of their background. However, this guide can be observed as just an introduction to the world of programming. With Scratch, it is easier to engage and to make content that is compatible with your needs while constantly improving your skills.

It is important to note that this guide doesn't assume that any of its readers has any prior experience or advanced knowledge about programming and that the level of mathematics used in examples is on a level no higher than high school. Still, learning something new takes time, and becoming good in programming is not something that can happen overnight. It takes time and practice and, of course, a lot of mistakes that will happen along the way. That is why you should arm yourself with patience and test as many different techniques that you can. Diversity will help you in multiple ways, and increase your ability to make more advanced projects.

As we already mentioned, this guide offers an approach that will influence your problem-solving skills while presenting programming concepts. The purpose of this approach is to stimulate imagination and make this kind of learning accessible to different kinds of readers. As you will see, the guide will focus more on concrete applications rather than Scratch's features. Also, all the examples that this guide covers are helpful with the diverse knowledge that Scratch can provide. That way, you can apply acquired skills to other fields in your life. There will be some exercises to encourage you to incorporate all that you have learned so far. Once you can solve different exercises on your own, it means that you have grasped the Scratch programming basics.

In the first few chapters of this guide, we will introduce Scratch and its tools for drawing and application. We will talk in more detail about geometric shapes and how can you draw them. Additionally, we will talk about the creation of simple applications yet enriched with media content. While this part will be dedicated to Scratch's unique features, the rest of the guide will be more focused on constructs that Scratch can support and program in general. After reading the following chapters, you should be able to recognize and use the environment in Scratch along with command blocks and simple program making. You should also be able to use the simplest motion commands while learning more about the possibilities of drawing in Scratch. Furthermore, there is a section that will teach you how to use graphics commands in Scratch and also how to add sound to your projects. This guide will help you understand procedures in Scratch while presenting them as a way to create programs of different structures. One of the main focuses will be variables and how you can use them since they are the most common feature in all interactive programs.

Every example and exercise in this guide should be used as a kind of pattern to create your own projects until you explore enough new options to create more advanced things. We hope that once you finish reading this guide, you can create a simple programming project that you want – on your own.

Chapter 1

Getting started with Scratch

If you ever thought about creating your own application, animation, tutorial or even your own computer game, Scratch should definitely be one of the programming languages you should be looking into. It provides you an interesting environment and offers different kinds of command blocks that you can use for the things you are interested in. In this first chapter, we will talk a little more about Scratch in general. The best thing is that everything that you make in Scratch can be stored directly on your computer or you can upload it on the Scratch website if you want to get feedback from other users.

Computer programs are usually just instructions that you use to tell your computer what you want it to do. The language that you use to do that is most frequently text-based, or we can say that you have to use some kind of cryptic English. For example, if you want your computer to display "Goodbye" there are several different ways to give that command to your computer depending on the programming language you want to use. If you use Java, the instruction will be system.out.print ("Goodbye");. Or if you want to give your command in the C++ language, for instance, it would be std::cout <<" Goodbye"<<std::endl; If you are a beginner, it can be

difficult to learn the rules and the ways that these programs use English syntax. That's where Scratch comes in and gives you something visual. Massachusetts Institute of Technology (MIT) Media Lab developed Scratch to make it easier for those interested in programming while making it more fun to learn. There aren't complicated wordy instructions to type in Scratch. However, you will find multimedia blocks that you'll need to connect if you want to make a program.

This might sound confusing, so we will use the example directly from the program to explain. When you open Scratch on your computer, one of the first figures that you'll see is a cat. In Scratch, that cat is called the sprite. You can give a series of commands to one sprite and it will understand and obey. The next thing you will see on your left side is the purple block that gives the command to the cat to say "Hello". This text is later displayed in a speech bubble. Multiple applications or animations that you'll make in Scratch will use more than one sprite, and these purple blocks will be used to make those sprites turn, talk, move, play some music, or even perform some mathematical tasks. Just imagine that you are playing with LEGO bricks rather than programming and you'll see that it isn't difficult to snap these colored blocks, which are actually codes. The script in Scratch refers to a stack of these color blocks that you get together. For example, the simplest way to see what it really is, would be to make your sprite change colors three or four times. You can put the pause of one second between each color change, and this set of connected commands to perform one complete action is a practical example of the script we mentioned above.

In this guide, we will use Scratch 2 for all explanations and examples. This version was released in 2013 and allows you to make projects on your browser so you don't even have to install the software. This is why we will mostly talk about the web interface of Scratch, and all the content of this guide will rely on it.

Program Environment in Scratch

Now that you can follow some of the basic things we can start using Scratch directly. Firstly, we will talk about the environment once you open the program. You can do that by going to the Scratch's official website http://scratch.mit.edu/. One of the links that you should see when you open this site in your browser is "Try it out" link when you click it, you should be redirected to the web editor interface that will allow you to create a new project.

The next thing that should appear on your display is one window with at least three panes. These panes should be the script tab (look on the right side of the window), the stage (look at the top left side of the window) and the sprite list, which should be on the bottom left side of the opened window. Script tab on the right side should also have script area and blocks as additional tabs along with the costume and sound sections.

If you make an account on the Scratch website and log in before you open the editor, you should be able to see one more additional feature called a backpack. It should be on the bottom right side of the window. The backpack consists of buttons that allow you to share the project you made while letting you use all of the sprites and scripts that exist in other projects available at the time. We will now discuss the three main panes and some of the additional sections in more detail.

The Stage

The Stage is a pane in which the sprite you use moves and interacts. It has a length of 480 steps and a height of 360 steps, and the center of this pane is marked with 0 on both the x and y coordinates. These (x, y) coordinates can be found at any point when you use the stage pane. The simplest way to see them is to just move the mouse cursor and you will see the numbers on the small display area that is located beneath the stage. Contrarily, above the stage, you will find a small bar that offers a few different controls. The first one is called the presentation mode and it is represented with an icon u. This icon enables you to hide all scripts and tools that you can use and spread up the stage across the entire display of your computer. The next control on the bar is the edit box represented with an icon v that shows the title of the project that you are working on at the moment. The bar above the stage also has icons for stopping and starting your program and they are represented as the standard X icon for closing and green flag for starting it.

Sprite List

On the sprite list pane, you fill find thumbnails and names for all the sprites that you plan to use in your project, and when you decide to start a new one, the stage pane will be white with one cat-shaped sprite. Some buttons appear above this pane. They have a function of adding new sprites into the current project. These new sprites can be added from four places such as Paint Editor (allows you to draw your own sprite costume), sprite library (every version of Scratch has one); you can add sprites from your computer (it's marked with an X icon) or from your computer camera (marked with the icon W). Every sprite that you add to the project you are working on will have its own costume, thus its own scripts and sounds. You can view all of their features by clicking on the thumbnails on the sprite list for each sprite individually, or you can just double click on the sprite, which belongings you want to view. If you decide to click on the thumbnail, the selected thumbnail will become outlined and highlighted in blue color.

Keep in mind that you can always access your sprites costumes, scripts and sounds also by clicking at the tabs that are above the script area too. The simplest way to do so is to use the right-click on your mouse cursor on your cat-shaped sprite and the pop-up menu will appear on the monitor. If you want, you can make endless copies of your sprite and Scratch automatically give them different names. If you, however, want to delete some of the sprites you've been using, you can do that by using the thumbnail marked with V (delete). On the other hand, if you want to export your sprite you can do that by using the local file option marked with the thumbnail W which will save your sprite as a .sprite2 file on your computer. This way you can use your own exported sprites to some other projects by clicking upload sprite from file button that appears above the stage along with the hide or show button that controls the appearance of your sprite on the display.

The sprite list not only shows the thumbnails that we mentioned but also the thumbnails for the stage pane on the left. The stage pane has its own, different, set of sounds and images, therefore its own scripts. It has a background image too, and this background image in Scratch is called the backdrop. Every time you start a new project in Scratch, the default setting of the stage is a white backdrop. However, you can always change that by adding other images as a backdrop image. If you click on the stage icon, the sprite list appears. It allows you to edit and view every background that you use, every sound implemented and additionally, allows you to edit all of the scripts that are associated with the project.

Blocks Tab

In version 2 of the Scratch, you can find ten categories in the block tabs. These categories can be referred to as palettes too, and they are motion, sound, data, looks, pen, control, events, operators, sensing, and more blocks in case you want to add additional ones to your project. Block tabs are designed to be in color so it is easier for you to find those who are related. Scratch in this version has over 100 blocks; however, some of them only appear if certain conditions are met. For instance, if you want to use blocks from the data category, you can't do that before you create a certain list or variable. Several components can be found in the blocks tab and the best way to explore them is to click on the block and just observe what it does.

For example, if you click on the motion palette and give the command to move, let's say, 20 steps, your sprite will move 20 steps on the stage pane. If you click on the palette again, it will move another 20 steps, and so forth. Also, if you want to instruct your sprite talk, you click on the looks category, then click on the "say hello" block and your sprite will have a speech bubble saying hello. When it comes to the length of the displaying the speech bubbles, you have an additional block in which you can put 2seconds, 5 seconds, etc. If you need help with blocks, there is a help screen that appears like a question mark icon on the toolbar. Once the "help" window is opened, you just click on the block you want to know more about. Not all blocks are the same; some of them need various arguments (or inputs) before they can instruct the sprite what to do next.

We will use the " move 20 steps" from the previous example because number 20, in this case, is an input. The block allows you to change the input by clicking on the white area and changing the number. You can put 15 steps or 30 steps; it depends on your own preference. Furthermore, there are blocks, like those who point in direction 90, that have drop menus and you can change your input by clicking on the down arrow and select one of the available options. When we talk about this particular command, once when you click it, the white area will appear, and you can just put the value that you want inside that white blocks while on the other "pull-down" menus you can only select one of the values which are already offered without changing them.

Scripts Area

If you want to make your sprite to do various interesting things you have to program it. Using Scratch, which means that you'll have to drag multiple blocks from the block tab and snap them together at the scripts area. When you want to move blocks in the scripts area, some indicators are highlighted in white color that tells you where you can put them to connect them properly to another block. Not every block can connect with every other that is why you have to follow which blocks are valid to snap together. This way Scratch eliminates potential errors that frequently happen when people use text-based program languages. One of the many benefits of Scratch is that you don't need to have complete scripts if you want to test them, you can just run them and see what they'll look like while building them. You just need to click on the script that you made so far and it will run even though you made it completely or just a part of it.

You don't even have to have all the blocks snapped to test them; you can just disassemble the stack and test each one individually which is very useful for later understanding of the longer scripts. If you want to move an entire stack rather than one block, just grab the top block and the whole stack will move in the pointed direction. If you want to detach some of the blocks, like a block in the middle, for example, and all of the blocks below it, you have to grab the preferred block and drag it. You can try this as many times as you need and with as many different stacks and blocks as you want. Scripts area enables you to build your project gradually, making one piece at a time by connecting smaller amount of blocks, testing them, and then combine them in a way that you want. This way you can make longer scripts as you advance with programming. Using smaller chunks of blocks and testing them allows you to see if everything is going to work like you intended to before you start making something more complicated. There is even an option of copying the stack of blocks from one sprite and use to another by dragging the stack from the script area to its other destination on the sprite list.

Costumes Tab

This tab enables you to change the look of your sprite. It is called changing the costume, but in fact, it is just an image. The costume tab has options that help you organize the look of your sprites so you can think of it as a kind of virtual costume. However, each sprite is limited to have just one costume at the time. Let's say that you want to change the costume of your cat-shaped sprite. You can easily do that by clicking at the costumes tab and choose one of the two costumes that are offered by default. The one that you choose will be highlighted and if you double-click it, it will become the current costume of your sprite. If you right-click on the costumes thumbnail, a drop menu will appear. There are three options in this menu: to duplicate the sprite, to delete it or to save it to the local file. If you click on the first option it will add a new, same costume that you copied, also, as its name suggests, the delete option is used if you want to delete the costume you previously selected. Finally, the last option enables you to save the preferred costume as a file and use it for other projects by clicking at the "upload costumes" button.

Sounds Tab

To make things even more interesting, Scratch allows your sprites to play sounds that can liven up your project. For example, you can use different sounds to express different moods of the sprite so others can see if the sprite is happy, or sad, or angry. If you make your sprite look like a bullet, for example, you can use different sounds to express if it missed or hit the target. There are several buttons in the sounds tab that can help you organize and incorporate sounds for sprites in your project. Also, there is a tool that allows you to edit sounds too which means that you can take your time and experiment with this feature as much as you want. Mostly, you will use one of the three buttons that are located at the top of this tab. Their functions are to enable you to record a new sound (you'll need a microphone for this one), to choose one of the already existing sounds from the Scratch library, or to import a sound directly from your computer. Keep in mind that Scratch accepts only two types of sound formats, which are WAV and MP3. You can try out getting some new ideas for your project by listening to some of the sounds that are already available in the Scratch library before importing or making something on your own. This way you will get more comfortable in using the program while exploring all of its options.

Backdrops Tab

We already mentioned the costumes tab. But, once you select one of the thumbnails on the Stage, the name of the costume tab in the sprite list changes to backdrops. The purpose of this tab is to help you organize all of the background images that can be found on stage pane. You can later change these images with the scripts you've made. For instance, if you want to make a game, you will need more than one background. Maybe you will use one backdrop with certain instructions for the beginning of the game and then switch it to another backdrop with some other instructions once when the game starts, and so on. Keep in mind that the backdrop tab and the costumes tab are identical. You can practice using the backdrop tab by clicking on the sprite list and select the XY grid while making it the default backdrop for your project. This grid will appear at the stage pane as a 2D Cartesian plane. This can be useful if you decide to work or practice with motion blocks. As with every other tab, you can repeat these steps while selecting different back drops as many times you like. It might even inspire you to make some new projects.

Sprite Info

If you want to view information about the sprites in your project you can do that by clicking on the icon that is located on the top-left edge of each sprite's thumbnail. Once you click the icon you will see the name of the sprite, the current position of the sprite (marked with x and y coordinates), the direction of the sprite, its visibility and the rotation of the sprite. Additionally, you will see if you can drag the sprite into the presentation mode.

The edit box that you can see at the top of the sprite info allows you to change the name of your sprite. You can sprite's name as many times as you want. On the other hand, X an Y letters represent the values that you use to determine the position of the sprite on the stage pane. Drag the sprite on the different spots on the stage and observe the numbers of these values and how they change. These values respond to the block movement and if you want to rotate the sprite you can do it by dragging the blue line that appears at the center of the rotation icon. There are three buttons for rotation. They are named: no rotate button; left-right flip button, and rotate button. These buttons control the appearance of the sprite's costumes when they change their direction.

To be able to understand better how these buttons work, you can create one script and click every button individually while the script is running. You can use the wait block which can be found in the control category or you can use the can block to check if the sprite can be moved to the presentation mode. This can be done by simply grabbing the sprite and dragging it to the presentation mode with the mouse cursor. The presentation mode is on when you check the box that will appear on the screen. Try dragging the sprite with this box unchecked too, and observe what happens. Sprite info also has the shadow checkbox, which enables you to hide or show the sprite in your project at the exact time that you want. There are also many ways to use hidden sprites and make them do a lot of tasks that can be useful and entertaining. Take your time to explore this feature.

Toolbar

Like many other programs, Scratch also has a toolbar. However, if you use a web interface, it will look different if you are signed in rather than being a guest user. If you want to delete sprites or to make more copies, you can use buttons " duplicate" or " delete";

both of these buttons are located at the toolbar. They can be used not only for sprites but for blocks, sounds, costumes, and scripts too. You will also find the "grow" button that makes your sprite bigger.

Contrarily, the "shrink" button will make it smaller. Both of these functions can be executed by clicking at the button first and then on the sprite that you want to use it on. Once when you finish with this, you can return your cursor to be an arrow by clicking on any part of the screen that is blank. If you have to change the language of the interface, you can do it by using the language bar. The toolbar also has the file menu, which allows you to create new projects, upload projects that you already have on your computer, to download the project you finished or to undo all the changes that you've done. If you use Scratch 2, you will notice that there is .sb2 extension for each file that you save. This way Scratch-made sure that you will distinguish its files from projects that you might have created in another Scratch version.

Finally, there is an edit menu that offers you actions such as "undelete" which returns the last thing you deleted whether it is a sprite, a block, a script, a costume or a sound. Additionally, you can shrink the stage and make the script area bigger using the "small stage" option. If you select turbo mode in the edit menu, you can increase the speed of the selected blocks. For instance, if you want to move a block a thousand times, it will take up to 70 seconds, but if you turn the turbo mode on, it will take only 0.2 seconds to perform the same action.

Paint Editor

This built-in Scratch feature allows you to create your own backdrops or costumes or edit the existing ones. This, however, doesn't mean that you can't use other editing programs to do so. Several resources provide more information about Scratch's paint editor. We would recommend the one named simply Scratch Paint Editor. It can be downloaded from the nostrach.com website. Still, there are only two features that you need to know more about as a beginner. You need to know how to set the center of an image and how to set a transparent color. We will discuss each of these features in the following text.

Every sprite tends to turn to a certain reference point. Regardless of the command being to move left or right, this center is always a center of the sprite's costume. That's where the setting of the image center feature comes in. There is a button on the upper-right corner of the paint editor that enables you to set the center of the costume (or an image). If you click this button, the crosshair will appear on the drawing area and the center point is actually a point of intersection of the axes that will appear on the editor. If you want to change this point, you need to shift it and drag it to the position that suits you. You can test out this feature by opening the file named "rotationcenter.sb2" and running it. This file has just one sprite along with one costume and one script connected to it. The costume center of this file is set in the middle. Try to determine the patterns once when you start running the application. When you establish the patterns, try editing the center of the costume and set it in the middle of the circle, for instance. Then run the application again and observe how the picture changed.

When you use more than one image, they may overlap and that one image covers some part of another. Also, the sprite that you use in your project may cover some parts of the stage pane. If you want to avoid that and to see the real appearance of the stage, and what it looks like behind the image, you will have to use the paint editor and make at least one part of that image transparent. The simplest way to do that is to go to the Color category, then find the square that has a diagonal red line over it, click it and use that "transparent" color to make invisible any part of the picture that you need. Transparent color can be observed as a "no color" sign that helps you remove all unnecessary parts of sprites or backdrops in the project.

Now that we have discussed some of the basic features that you can see once you open Scratch for the first time, we will make that knowledge useful by going through a concrete assignment. We will see how we can make a simple game in Scratch by incorporating everything that we've learned so far.

The Game Example

In this example, we will try to create a single-player game. The game isn't complicated and its purpose is to make players move a paddle to keep the tennis ball from hitting the floor. As you can suggest, the game we will try to make using Scratch is based on the classic game that many of us played as children, the arcade game named Pong.

The concept is simple; the ball has to start at the top of the stage pane and to move down. The angle of the ball's movement is random which means that it can bounce off the edges of the stage on its way toward the bottom of the display. The role of the player is to move the paddle using the mouse and send the ball back up. The paddle moves horizontally and if the player fails to send the ball up and it touches the stage, the game ends. Of course, we will need several steps to create the game, but first, we need to open a new project and to remove a cat-shaped sprite. You can do that by selecting "file 4new" on the Scratch menu and the new project will open. Cat sprite is deleted by selecting " delete" from the drop menu once that you right-click on it.

The first step is to prepare the backdrop. If you want to command the game to recognize when the ball missed the paddle, you'll need to mark the bottom of the stage pane with a color of your choice. The preferred color can be selected from the sensing category, and then you apply it to the block, which will detect if the ball touched the color during the game or not. When you finish this, click once again on the stage to return to it and then go again to the backdrops tab. Use the drawing option to draw a thin rectangle (that resembles a paddle) that will be positioned at the bottom of the backdrop.

The next step is to try adding the paddle and the ball. To do this, you need to add the paddle sprite to your project first. Click at the "new sprite" button that appears above the sprite list. As you suggest, the paddle is actually a thin rectangle like the one that we mentioned in the first step. That is why you should repeat that step and draw the same rectangle that will represent the paddle. You can color the paddle once when you finish it using any color that you want while setting the center at the approximate middle of the rectangle. You should name the sprite with something that will explain its function. In this case, the most logical name of the sprite that you added is "paddle". This image should have its y coordinate set to be 120 in value. Now, you managed to put a paddle into your game but you still need a ball that is supposed to bounce through the stage pane. The best way to add the ball is to click on the Scratch library and choose one of the existing sprites and import it into your game. When you click the library, the dialog will appear with a thing category inside. Chose that category and select a tennis ball sprite that will immediately be added to the project. Similarly, as with the paddle name, you can just name this new sprite "ball", since that is its primal description and role. To prevent any unpredictable occurrences, you should save the project to your computer before you start making scripts for the game. You can do that by selecting file downloads and just select in which folder you want to save it. You can name it "pong" for example, and it will appear on your computer as pong.sb2. If you made an account and you were logged in while making the game, you can also save your progress on the Scratch server or the cloud. Regardless of the place in which you want to store your files, keep in mind that the best way to protect your work is to save the things you do as often as you can. Now you have the two most essential sprites for your game.

The step that follows these initial sprites is to decide how the game will start and to make these sprites move. Since you are the designer of the game, you can choose how players will start their new rounds. For instance, you can make them start the game only if they press a certain key. Also, it can start by clicking at one of the sprites or even clapping if the player has a proper webcam that can use. Still, in this example, we will use the green flag that you will see above the stage because it is the most popular option in Scratch. The way of making this work is very straightforward. Every script that starts with this green flag will trigger the block when clicked and they will run whenever you press that particular button. When the script starts, the flag becomes bright green, and that color stays until the script is finished.

So once you click the green flag you go to the XY block and set the vertical position of the paddle to -120 degrees. You should double-check this before you continue because it can happen that you accidentally moved the value with the mouse. The goal is to make the paddle that you've made hover above the rectangle (colored pink for example) at the bottom of the stage pane. If you made a thicker rectangle just adapt its position number so it can work in your design without problems. When you do all this, the script will automatically turn the "forever" block, which will constantly check the position of the mouse during the game. Try moving the paddle back and then forth while matching the x position of the mouse with the x position of the paddle. Then try running the script by clicking the green flag we mentioned before, but this time try moving your mouse up and down. If everything is ok, the paddle should follow the movement of the mouse. When you finish testing this part click the stop icon that is located next to the green flag and stops the script.

Another script that you need to make is the one for the ball sprite and it is a little longer than the one you had to make for the paddle. To avoid confusion, we will divide the script into smaller parts. The first thing you need to do is the same as for the paddle, you have to click the green flag above the sprite and the ball will start moving which means that now we can add the script that suits the game. We will move the ball sprite to the upper part of the stage pane and command it to go down at a random angle. To do this, you need to pick the random block button marked with V from the operators' category. Like before, the script automatically uses the forever block (marked with the letter w) and moves the ball all over the stage pane while bouncing it off the edges of the displayed area. Try testing everything you've done so far by clicking the green flag. If you did everything correctly, the ball should be moving using the zigzag pattern and the paddle that you previously scripted should follow the moves you make with the mouse. You can try out replacing values that are inside the moving block and make the game harder by increasing the number that's inside. When you decide what kind of level you want for your game just click stop and then you can continue designing your game.

The next part of the script that you'll have to write is how to make the ball that points down bounce off the paddle that you move with the mouse. It is actually very simple if you modify the forever block that you have in the previous part of the script. Adjust the block so the ball can travel up when it hits the paddle. You will do that by commanding the ball that when it touches the paddle goes at the random direction. In this example, we will say that the space for this should be between -30 and 30 on the Y scale. Now, when the forever block starts running for the next round of the game the moving block will execute the command which will cause the ball sprite to travel up. If you want to test this, again, click the green flag; and once when you make sure that the ball is really bouncing off of the paddle in the way you expected it to, you can use stop icon to pause the script. At this point, the only thing that needs to be coded is ending the game if the paddle doesn't prevent the ball from touching the bottom of the stage pane. You can add this script to the ball sprite before or after the previous block that you scripted. The moving block can be found in the sensing category while the stop block can be found at the control palette. It should work like this: you click the mouse over the square that is colored and the mouse cursor should change from an arrow to the hand. Move the hand cursor and click above the pink rectangle that appears at the bottom of the stage and keep in mind that the square that you are using should match the color of the rectangle.

If you click "stop all block" it will execute the action that its name suggests and stop running every script in every sprite that you have in your project. This means that neither the ball nor the paddle is an exception. With this, you have your first basic game that is fully functional. Still, you should test it a few more times just to make sure that all parts of the game are working properly. If everything is fine, you achieved one of the main goals of the Scratch- to make a complete game using a very small amount of the code. This is one of the things that makes Scratch more accessible than other program languages.

The final thing that you can do is to make your game more fun with sound. You can do that by adding noise every time that you hit the ball with the paddle. The simplest way to add sound is to double-click at the ball sprite that is located on the stage, then select the sounds tab. In the beginning, the best thing is to use some of the sounds from the Scratch's library so you click the "choose sound from library" button and then add one of the sounds that you like to the sprite by clicking OK. After you finish this, go to the scripts tab again and insert the sound block from the sound category. Keep in mind that you should test the game after this, and if everything is alright you will hear a sound that you chose (a short "pop" sound for example) every time you touch the ball with the paddle. With this final touch, you have completed your first game using Scratch as the programming language. Of course, you can always add more features to it by adding two or more balls, for example, the process is the same so the only thing you need is the time to explore and experiment further. The following text will be more dedicated to the types of blocks that Scratch offers, and some of those blocks were intensively used to build up the game from our example.

An Overview of Scratch blocks

We will use this section to talk more about the blocks that are available in Scratch. You will learn more about their names and their role in the program. The purpose is to try to define terms that you might be unknown to you and that will be used throughout this guide. This part of the guide can be a part that you'll return to whenever you feel stuck and you need to remind yourself of certain expressions. The version of Scratch that we use as a reference in the guide offers four types of blocks. These blocks are the function blocks, the command blocks, the control blocks, and the trigger blocks. We have already met with most of them in the previous text.

The control blocks and the command blocks are also known as the stacks. They have notches on their tops or they have bumps on their bottoms. As their name suggests, these blocks can be snapped together into the stacks.

Trigger blocks, on the other hand, are better known as hats because they have rounded tops. These blocks are usually placed at the top of each stack and they connect scripts with events. They wait for an event such as a mouse click, for instance, and after the event happens they run the blocks that are located beneath them. If we use our "pong" game as an example, the trigger block, in that case, is the green flag that you have to click whenever you want to start the scripts that you made running.

Function blocks are sometimes called the reporters, and these blocks aren't round and they have neither bumps nor notches. Function blocks are actually inputs to other blocks rather than a layer of an actual script. The shape of the block is an indicator of the data that you can expect them to return. For instance, if you choose a function with the pointed ends, it will report if something that you did is true or false, or if you click on the function block with the rounded end, it will report number that you used in the project or the strings used in it. Some of these blocks come with a checkbox. If this box is checked, a new, smaller window appears on the monitor and shows the current value of the function that is reported. For example, you can select a sprite and once that the checkbox appears you can check it on the position block (marked x) that is located in the motion palette. If you try dragging the sprite around the stage pane the box and the values should move and change along with the sprite.

Functions and Arithmetic Operators in Scratch

Even though we won't talk as much as we should in this section, we will, however, cover the most important things that you need to understand about the functions and arithmetic operations that Scratch supports. If you, for example, need to calculate something and you don't have a calculator anywhere around, you can just make one using the program using the blocks from the operators' palette.

The operators' palette offers blocks that can perform all of the four basic arithmetic operations. Whether you want to add, subtract, multiply or divide numbers, you can do that by running these blocks, and since they produce numbers they can be used as inputs for all other blocks that support numeric values.

Scratch doesn't only support the basic operations but also the modulus operator (mod), which allows you to return the remainder of the two numbers' division. For instance, if you put 10mod3, the return is one because when you divide 10 by three the remainder of dividing these two numbers is number 1. The most common usage of this operator is when you want to test if one whole number (or integer) is divisible by other, smaller numbers. If the modulus is 0, it means that the bigger number can be divided with a smaller number. Modulus allows you to see if the number that you'll get is even or odd. Additionally, Scratch also supports round operator, which has the purpose of rounding decimals to the nearest number that is whole. For example, if you get 3.1 the round operator will round it to the number 3 if the number is 2.6 the round operator will round it to 3 and so forth.

When you start using Scratch more often, at some point you will have to know how to generate random numbers. This is especially important if you want to create more games or some simulations. Scratch has random blocks that are designed specifically for that. Random blocks create outputs, which are, as their name suggests, random numbers each time you click on them. These blocks have editable white areas inside in which you can enter a range for the number you need. Scratch will always choose the number that is between the values that you've set, including them. Keep in mind that you will get different outputs if you set ending values to be 1 to 2 or 1 to 1.0. If you choose the first version, you will get the whole numbers, which are, in this case, 1 or 2. Still, if you choose the other version, the random pick will be a decimal value between 1 and 2. Whenever you set a decimal number to be the limiting input, the output that you get will also be a decimal.

Other than these basic operations, Scratch can support various mathematical functions. If you put different blocks together, the program can perform up to 14 mathematical functions that will appear in the drop menu. Some of these functions are logarithms, trigonometry, calculating the square root of a number or finding the exponential function of it. If you want to learn more about this Scratch feature, the best thing is to use the Mathematical Functions manual that can be found in the support documents of the program. This file contains more extensive coverage of all functions that you can perform in Scratch and how to combine blocks to do so.

In this first chapter, we overviewed all of the most important categories and features that appear in Scratch's program environment. You had the opportunity to read more about the different elements of the web user interface and we even talked about the complete process of making a game. Through these previous sections, you could explore how you can use Scratch to build your own calculator that can support different operations and functions. At this point, we can say that you are familiar with the most basic information that you need to make some more complicated scripts. Still, it is a long way before you can write advanced programs. In the next chapter, we will talk more about some skills that will improve your programming ability in Scratch, but before that, here are few examples that you can use for practicing the things that you've learned so far.

Firstly, you can view the mathematical operations like 8x8, 88x88, 888x888, etc. and determine if there is a pattern in these products. To check your answers use the "say" command and calculate the results with Scratch.

Secondly, you can try to calculate the values of the following expressions: $2 + (3 \times 5)$; $(12 / 3) - 4$; $8 + (9 \times 3) - 5$; $(3 + 4) \times 5$; $6 + (3 \times (8 - 5))$; $(12 - 6) \times (3 + 2) / 3$; $6 \times (6 + 5) - 3 \times (2 + 4) (7 + 13) \bmod 5$; $4 \times (14 \bmod 4$; $6 + (18 \bmod 6) - 4$. Once when you calculate this, use the "say" command again, and check your results in Scratch.

The third task that you can do to check how Scratch operates with math functions is to try calculating values like the sine of 60° for example, or the square root of 45, and then check if those values are the same in Scratch when you run the "say" command. You can also try rounding some numbers or creating functional blocks that will calculate the average of numbers like 80, 85, 88, etc. Each time, you will use the "say" command to display the result.

If you want to try some more complicated assignments, you can try creating function blocks that will convert Fahrenheit to Celsius. Let's say that you want to convert 70 Fahrenheit into Celsius. Keep in mind that Celsius = (5/9) x (Fahrenheit – 32). Or you can try creating function blocks that will calculate the area of a trapezoid. Let's say that the height of that trapezoid is 5/7 foot and that the basis of the trapezoid has lengths of 4/8 and 21/8 foot. Remember that the formula should be A= 0.5 x (b1 +b2) x h. In this case, b1 and b2 refer to the lengths of the basis and h refers to the height of the trapezoid.

If you want to create blocks that involve formulas from physics rather than just math, you can try creating a function block that will calculate the force that you'd need to accelerate a 2.300kg car 4m/s2. Reminder: the formula for calculating the force is mass multiplied with acceleration.

Chapter 2

Drawing and Motion in Scratch

Now that you are familiar with the web interface in Scratch we will advance and talk about more programming tools that you can use. Through this chapter, we will discuss pen commands and motion in Scratch, we will explore the animation feature and see how sprites can be animated and moved around the stage pane; we will talk about drawing patterns whether they are geometric, artistic or something else, and we will try to explain why cloning tool is a valuable asset that you can use while programming.

This part of the guide focuses more on the creative part of the Scratch programming language, which means that we will mostly use the computer graphics rather than the operational patterns that stand behind them.

Motion Commands in Scratch

Once when you start making your own animated programs or games you will need to know how to use blocks from the motion category. These blocks command the sprites to move around the stage pane while allowing you to set the exact way and the spot in which you want to move the sprite. This section will discuss in more detail how you can give these particular instructions and place the sprites on a certain spot or just make them move in a particular direction.

Absolute Motion Commands

If you remember from the previous chapter, the most common proportion of the stage panel is 480x360 grids in a shape of rectangular. The center of the stage is set to be at the point labeled 0, 0. In Scratch, you have four commands that are considered to be absolute motion commands. Those are: glide to; go to; set x to and set y to. These instructions tell the sprite exactly where they need to be positioned in the grid that we mentioned above. If you want to find out more about other blocks in this category you can use Scratch tips that are located at the right side on the scripts panel. In case you can't find it, the easiest thing is to click on the question mark near the project editor and find all the additional information that you need.

For a better understanding of these commands, let's say that you want to make the airplane sprite move and hit the circle-shaped target that you placed on the grid. The location of the target is positioned at 250 on x coordinate and 200 at y coordinate. The simplest way to do this is to find the "go to" block and use x and y coordinates to tell your sprite where it should move to. Since you still haven't programmed your airplane to hit the target, it will just move along the line that is connected to its current position which means that it will move along from the point 0,0 up to the point with the coordinates 250, 200. If you want to slow down your airplane sprite you can do that by using the glide command instead of going to because they are almost identical, however, the glide command allows you to set the time you want for the airplane to reach the intended target. This leads us to our next step- making the plane reach the target.

Hitting the target can be set by independently changing the x and y coordinates for the airplane sprite. It uses the same principle as we used when we were talking about setting x coordinates in our Pong game example. The thing is that you can always access the position of the sprite in the coordinate system using the scripts area and if you want to display that information on the stage you can just use the reporter blocks that we also mentioned before. And if you click the checkboxes that appear next to the reporter blocks the values of the sprites on the stage will appear.

Keep in mind that all motion commands work using a sprite center as a reference. We already mentioned that you can set this center using the paint editor built-in Scratch. For example, you can send a sprite to the position with the XY coordinates 150, 150 and then move the sprite so its center becomes positioned at those coordinates rather than default 0,0. This means that you can experiment a lot with the sprites and its movements but always pay attention to their center.

Relative Motion Commands

For relative motion, we will use the airplane and the target again, but this time we will suppose that you can't see the exact coordinates of the sprites so you can't determine their precise position. This means that you have to use another system to tell the airplane where and how to move to hit the target. For example, you can make a command that the sprite needs to move four steps then to turn left and move 5 steps forward, or something similar. Once that you use commands like "turn" or " move" it means that you are using the relative motion commands in Scratch. The first one that we used above, the " move" command, tells your sprite to go up while the "turn" command caused it to go left in the process. These motions depend on the current location of the sprite. If you want to make your sprite go towards a specific direction you can do that by using the point in the direction command and choose right, left, up or down. One-click at the desired direction from the drop menu that appears and your sprite will follow. If you want to command some other directions you need to add a numeric value to the white area of the edit box. In this case, you can even use negative numeric values. For instance, try typing 25 or -210, both of these numbers will point your sprite to move northeast on the stage panel.

Note that you can find the current direction of the sprite in the info area along with other relevant information. Additionally, you can determine the position of the sprite by clicking the checkbox that appears next to the direction block in the motion category. It will show you exactly where the sprite is located on the stage panel. Now that we explained the basics of the relative motion commands, we can see how they work on the practical example. Keep in mind that like with the absolute motion, there are for main relative motion commands. These commands are: turn and move that we already mentioned, and additionally we have change x by and change y by commands. So, if we want to move the airplane, we will determine its current location first. Then we will align the center of the plane with the center of the stage by using the blocks in the editor that we mentioned above. After this, we will use another block to command our airplane sprite to go up, and then the third block to command the sprite to turn 60 degrees clockwise for example. Then we can command the sprite to move further making 80 steps forward and turn back 30 degrees counterclockwise before stopping at that position.

Costumes and Directions

Sprite's costume position is unknown to the direction command. Let's say that we use two sprite costumes that we drew. The first one is a costume of a bird, and the second one is an insect that faces up that bird. Now, try commanding both sprites using the block that point right (or direct 90 degrees). You will see that neither bird nor the insect sprite turned even though the insect faces right. This happened because although the direction "right" is referred to as turning 90 degrees the direction actually pointed at the costume's original orientation that we left in the paint editor when we drew the sprites. If you want to make sure that costumes follow the commands properly, you need to draw costumes that will be compatible with their position in the paint editor and the stage panel. Your project may require only horizontal or vertical movement from their current position. This is where you use XY blocks and you change the numeric value in them. For example, you want to move the airplane sprite to the center of the stage panel. Firstly, you can change the X coordinates and command your sprite to go 60 steps (in this case on the right) and then change Y value into 60 too, making your sprite move up 60 steps up. All other commands for motion in Scratch are based on the same principle, and if you want to trace how the sprite moved you can start by determining its final destination and retracing the steps.

Other Motion Commands that you can use

Since we already mentioned most of the motion commands that Scratch offers, there are only four left to mention. These commands are bounce; if on edge; the second type of go-to block and set rotation style.

Rotation styles were previously mentioned in the first chapter along with the bounce command that we used to write the proper code for the ball sprite in the Pong game example. So, to see the two remaining commands in action we will also try to make a simple program in which we'll make the cat chase the ball instead of the ball bouncing off of the paddle. So, we have two sprites- cat and the ball, thus we have two scripts that we need to make. Same as before, firstly you need to click the green flag and the ball-shaped sprite will follow the mouse cursor. The cat sprite should point continuously in the direction of the ball and you can use the glide block command to achieve that. Of course, you will have to use the forever block from the control category and mouse XY blocks from the sensing category to make everything work properly. Take your time and try doing this as many times as you need, and if you have any additional questions, don't forget to click the question mark.

Easy Draw and Pen Commands in Scratch

In this section, we will explore the pen palette and discuss in more detail how you can make your sprite leave a trace of its motion that can be seen. The motion commands that we explained before can move the sprite in the wanted direction at any point of the stage grid, however, there is a way of seeing the path that the desired sprite will travel. To make this happen, you will need to know how to use a pen command in Scratch. The thing that we didn't mention before is that every sprite on the stage has an invisible pen connected to it. This pen can be located either up or down, depending on the sprite. If the pen is below the sprite, the path will be drawn along with the sprite movement. Contrarily, the sprite can travel from place to place on the grid without leaving any trace of its movements. The pen command allows you to control the size of the pen, the color of the path and if you want to use a shade or not.

For more tips, you can open the Tips window, find the house icon and click on the pen for all commands and their brief descriptions. You will find the scripts that demonstrate most of those commands, so you can practice by re-creating them, running them and try to describe all of the outputs that you get out of them. Remember that you need to set the pen to be located below the sprite if you want to see its path. The easiest way to do that is to find the appropriate block in the control palette.

We can look into more details for some of the pen commands and then try to create a simple application that will draw pictures while the sprite moves. This time we will use the arrow keys to move the sprites.

Let's say that every time you press the down arrow (↓), the sprite will go back 20 steps, and if you press the up arrow (↑), the selected sprite will go 20 steps forward. Also, each time you use left and right key arrows (←)(→), the sprite will move either 20 degrees left or 20 degrees right. This means that if you want your sprite to turn 120 degreed left, for example, you will need to press the left arrow 6 times.

Once again, let's try making a practical example to test out all of these commands. Firstly, open a new project the same way you did when you tried making a Pong game. Then replace the cat-shaped sprite with any other sprite that you want, the only requirement is that the costume has to show clearly in which direction is pointing to. You can choose something from the animal folder for instance. As before, you find the costumes tab, then click at the chosen costume from the library option and select whatever costume you want. The next step is to add scripts to that costume. Use the events palette to create the command blocks for four keys and program space key to have a function of blocking the script. Once you finish this, click the green flag, as usual, the script will start running and the sprite will move to the center of the stage panel and the sprite will point up. This is where you need to set the pen's size and color have to be set and you need to make sure that the pen is positioned below the sprite. Now, the sprite is ready to draw the path while moving, and all other drawings were deleted. And when you want to make a new drawing, just clear the stage and start the next one using the green flag. You can use keyboard arrows to instruct the sprite to draw whatever shape you like. Try different combinations, or add some variation using different colors and sizes of the pen. Tip: you can use keyboard shortcuts to make pen wider (press W) or narrower (press N).

The Power of Script Replication

Programs that we tried to create so far have been simple, but as you start to make more complicated scripts you will often have to replicate the same stack of blocks that you snapped together, even multiple times in a row. Making double scripts makes the script longer, thus harder to comprehend. This means that at some point, it might be difficult to even experiment with it. And if you have to change any of the values in the code, you have to make the same change in every copy of the code that you've made so far. This is where the repeat command comes in and helps you with this kind of problem. You can find it at the control palette. For instance, let's say that you want to draw a rectangle and you want it to follow repetitive instructions. These instructions can be to move 30 steps forward and then turn 120 degrees clockwise for example. Then the sprite can move the next 30 steps and rotate 120 degrees clockwise again. Then repeat the same thing once again, and so forth. This means that you'll have to use scripts that implement these repetitive instructions. Note that the sprite moves the same way three times in a row. You can avoid adding the same blocks all over again and use the repeat block which will command the sprite to move the way you want to form as many times that you need. Repeat blocks help you understand better what happens inside the program and how to utilize scripts even when they are long.

You can practice this by modifying the shape of the sprite, therefore its scripts. For the beginning, the easiest way is to draw squares or other polygons. Keep in mind that you can substitute any number (only the whole numbers) in these modified script versions when it comes to the number of sizes. This way you can determine the shape of your sprite. Additionally, you can change any value for changing the length of the sprite and that way you can control its size. Also, you can use repetitive scripts to make multiple polygons of the same size. If you want to position them differently, you can do that by pointing the green arrow to the place you want to place them. Finally, you can use the file named polygon.sb2 and add different values to the number of side field. When you run the file pay attention to what happens with the sprites on the stage panel.

Rotated Squares in Scratch

If you tend to create more artistic forms, you can also do that by using a certain sequence and repetitive patterns. For instance, you can make a squared drawing and rotate it 14 times for example. Use the block that will place the pen below the sprite and initialize it. Afterward, you should use the repeat block that is located out of the sprite and command it to repeat the drawing 14 times. The additional command is that every time that the pen is inside this loop it should draw a squared path and when it rotates to the left (let's say 30 degrees) it should turn right (or left if you prefer) and prepare to draw the next square-shaped path of the sprite. Note that you can change the number of repetitions and the size of the angles and adjust it to your own preferences. You can experiment with different values in both categories and observe what happens with the sprite and its movements.

How to use more complicated sprite shapes in Scratch

In the previous section, you learned about repeat blocks and how to use simple shapes even in more complex code patterns. Since you are now familiar with that concept, in the following text we will use a little more complicated strategy. We will try to make new costumes in the paint editor and use stamp blocks that will help us make multiple copies of that sprite on the stage panel. For better understanding, let's immediately start by drawing a sprite in the shape of the windmill.

Firstly, try drawing the shape of the flag in the paint editor and use it as a sprite in your new Scratch project. Then you set the center of your costume (we already discussed the importance of this in the first chapter). The center should be at the lower tip of the drawn flag so the sprite can rotate around that point. The next step is using the script that will draw the windmill shaped sprites. You set the command to the repeat block that it has to stamp the copy of a costume for nine times for example. The next command is that every copy has to be a sprite rotated for a certain number of degrees (let's say 45 in this case) before it appears on the stage panel. To make this script functional, you need to use a block for rotation style in combination with the rotation style set. Without doing that, the flags won't be able to flip while they rotate. You can also try out changing the color effects by choosing some of the blocks from the looks palette. These blocks allow you to chose different graphics such as fisheye or whirl for example. When you open the windmill.sb2 file you can add one of these commands into the repeat block. Choose other effects if you want and experiment with them to make more cool patterns that you can later apply on some other projects.

If you want to explore more about these Scratch features, you can use the information from "extra resources" - a package that can be downloaded from the nostrach.com website. Drawing geometric shapes explained there is far more detailed than you can find here since this is primarily a beginner's guide. If you, however, want to try drawing more complicated shapes such as trapezoids, kites, parallelograms, etc, feel free to try it for as long as you want!

New project examples that you can complete in Scratch

Now that we already went through some more complicated things we can try developing more completed programs. Instead of creating one, this time we will focus on creating two different applications that will help you incorporate everything that you've learned so far, especially regarding the pen blocks and motion blocks.

Even if some things that we will mention didn't appear in the topics that we covered so far, we will explain them in some of the next chapters. Also, if you think that you need more information, you can use the website that we always use as a reference and find everything you need (the website is nostrach.com).

The first application

The first program that we will try to complete is one more game with a simple concept: the player has to use key arrows to move the sprite and collect bags of gold. The goal of the game is to collect as many bags as you can and if you can't grab the bag within the three seconds, for example, that bag disappears and another one appears on some other location on the grid. The locations of the bags should be random in this case. You will have to open the file named money_nocode.sb2, and even though that the file doesn't have automatic scripts that you can run immediately, you will create them and this file has everything you need once that you write the appropriate script for your game.

So, you need to write the script that will move the sprite to the certain coordinates and point them to the direction that you want. In this case, we will set the coordinates to be -40,/40 and the sprite will be pointed to the right. The remaining four scripts should respond to each arrow key that player uses separately. This means that when a player presses a key, the scrip that corresponds with that arrow changes the direction of the sprite while playing a sound that you can insert additionally (as you already know, the sound blocks are located in the sound palette and the best choice is to use sounds from the Scratch library for now). The arrow should also have a numeric value added to its direction, which means that if a player presses left arrow the sprite will move left and go 50 steps for instance. The next motion command that you will incorporate is the command in which the sprite has to bounce off of the stage panel. Let's say that 50 steps of the sprite are approximately the same as one square on the stage panel grid. If we use this analogy, it means that every time the player presses and arrow key the sprite will move for one square rather than 50 steps.

Once you are done writing this part of the game you should try it out a few times. If the sprite moves around the stage every time that you (or in this case the player) press the keyboard arrow it means that you've done everything correctly so far. The next phase is to make the gold sprite and its script, which should also start when you click on the green flag. This script is supposed to move the gold sprite around the stage panel and to track how many bags the player collected. Here is one new thing- tracking the number of collected gold bags requires a variable that is named "score" and you can find it at the data category.

Note that all labels that are similar to the score that we have in this application are called variables. These labels enable you to store information that you can use later in your projects. We will talk more about them in the next chapters. When a player starts a game, he doesn't have any bags collected, which means that his score is zero, thus we set the variable to start with that number. The next step is starting a loop that will repeat for let's say 30 times. This automatically means that the number of bags that the player will see and try to collect is 30. Every time that you run the loop a new gold sprite appears and gives the time you selected to the player to collect it. Since we already said that the locations of the gold bags are random, it is important to note that with every collected bag the player's score increases. To make bags appear in random locations you need to set their position values as you like. Let's say that the positions that you entered are -200, - 140, -80, 220, etc, since all of these numbers are spaced 50 steps apart you can find the position of the bags if you calculate it using the following pattern: x= -200 + (0x50); x= -200 + (1x50); x= -200 + (2x 50); x= -200 + (3x 50); x= -200 + (4x50); x= -200 + (5x 50) and so on.

The same principle applies if you want to calculate the value of Y. This means that we can set the x position of the gold sprite using random numbers between 0 and 4 in this case, multiply those numbers by 50 and adding the result to -200.

To create an x set for your application you need to construct the x block similarly. The bag of gold has to appear at a random location but remember that you need to give the player some time to catch it. The amount of time that you set will define the level of the game making it harder or easier to play. If you want to add a tracking time feature you need to reset the script's timer to 0. This timer is built in the Scratch already so you don' need to program it separately. Once you reset the timer, it will wait until the time exceeds the limit that you gave or until the player catches the golden bag. Regardless of the condition that is met, the block named "wait until" will allow the running script to execute "if/then" block. This means that every block that is set inside the conditioned "if/then" block will activate only if the condition that you specified is met. In this case, the mentioned block will run if the player grabs the golden bag changing the score that you imported from the data pallet and adding one point per bag to it.

With this final step, you have completed this application. Click the green flag to test it a few more times, just in case you need to make some corrections.

Before we continue talking about the second application in this part of the guide, we will say a few things about the Scratch timer first. As we already mentioned, Scratch has a built-in timer that can record and save the amount of time that has passed since you started the program. For example, when you open Scratch in your web browser and the web interface appears, the timer is set to zero. This number will increase each second for as long as you keep Scratch opened in the browser. If you want to block the timer you will have to go to the sensing palette and find its current numeric value. Once you open this feature the checkbox will appear on the screen and it will allow you to show or hide the monitor of the timer block on the stage panel. If you want to reset the timer you have to use the reset block, which will return the timer to zero and then again start counting new time. Scratch's timer can work even if the project stops running at some point.

The second application
In this section, we will try to complete another game. The concept of this game is similar to the first one because it's based on the player catching the apples. Still, in this version, the apples will appear at horizontal positions at the top of the stage panel. They

will appear at random positions and at random times. The player has to catch the apples using the cart sprite before the apples hit the ground. Each apple that a player catches is worth one point.

In the beginning, it might seem that you will need too many sprites that have almost identical scripts because there are a lot of apples. However, the version of the Scratch that we use in this guide has something called a cloning feature. With this feature, you can create as many copies of the sprites as you need. For the game that you are trying to create now, use one apple-shaped sprite and then create the amount of the clones that you want. The next step is to open the file named catchapples_nocode.sb2, which has setups with variables without the scripts like in the previous game. Setting the score variable is based on the same principle as with the golden bag game so you can use it to keep track of the number of apples that the player collects. Still, before you do that, you have to make a script that will correspond with the cart sprite.

Like with every other script, everything starts with the green flag. When you click on it, move the cart-shaped sprite to the bottom of the stage panel. The script should constantly check the left and the right arrow and if they move along with the cart. You can use different values for the number of steps you want to move the cart with one pressing of an arrow. The next phase is the cloning process. You can start by adding the appropriate script to the apple-shaped sprite and then run it by clicking the green flag.

Similarly, with the first game, the score at the beginning is zero, since the player still didn't catch any apples. To make the sprites visible, you will have to go to the looks palette and choose the show block. Then you have to start the repeat block that will loop the sprite for the number of times that you have set. Every time that one loop passes, the apple sprite moves to another randomly set horizontal position at the top of the stage panel.

It then should call a block from the control palette named "create clone", thus the sprite should clone itself the necessary number of times. After every clone, the sprite waits for a short, randomly set time, and then continues with the next round using the repeat block. When the sprite finishes all the rounds that you set (let's say that your command was to make 20 apples) a new script appears and uses the hide blocks from the looks category to hide the apple sprite. Still, if you run the application at this point, you will only get 20 apples at the random positions on the horizontal line of the stage panel because you still haven't instructed the clones what they need to do.

When you go to the control palette and choose the clone block you need to set a script that each clone will execute. For example, you can set that each clone (or in this case apple) goes down 20 steps and then checks if it missed the cart or not. If the apple detected that is touching the cart, the script will run as the apple was caught. This action increases the player's score accordingly and plays a sound (remember to set one using the sounds from the Scratch sound library) and once when it's caught it deletes itself because its work is done. On the other hand, if the apple doesn't touch the cart and falls somewhere else, it should play a different sound so the player can recognize that he missed and then again- delete itself. When the apple travels from the top of the stage panel to its bottom it means that it's neither missed nor caught – it's falling, which means that you must include the forever block, which will run in this situation. Once when you are finished with making apple-shaped sprites fall, you have successfully completed another application. As usual, you should test it by clicking the green flag and observing if everything goes as planned. You can always add more features, change colors, values, sounds, and many other things that can make the game more interesting.

A Little Bit on Cloned Sprites

All of the sprites used in Scratch can copy themselves or other sprites by using the block named "create clone" that we mentioned in the previous section. It is important to remember that even the stage panel can clone sprites on the same principle and using the same block. Keep in mind that the cloned sprite has all of the characteristics of the original one, which means that it keeps the original position, costume, direction, pen size and color, visibility, even the graphic effects and all other features that you can think of. The original sprite is also known as the master sprite and every clone inherits the same script like the master sprite. Let's make two clones of the master sprite. If you press the space bar all of the sprites (now it's three of them: master sprite + 2 clones) will execute the same command. If pressing the spacebar means that the master clone has to rotate 30 degrees, in this case, all of the sprites will do the same because they all have the same command in their scripts. Pay attention when you use clone blocks if the script doesn't start immediately when you press the green flag or it can happen that the block will create more clones. For example, if you press the spacebar one time, and the command is to make two clones when this button is pressed, the second time you press the spacebar you will have four clones (or five sprites in total: one master and four clone sprites). This happens because the master sprite always responds to the spacebar key that commands it to create a clone, and since its clones have the same script, the second pressing of the button is a command that they make a clone of their clone and so forth. The number of clones always grows exponentially but you can limit them by cloning only those, which have green flag clicked the box next to them.

This chapter had a purpose to explore the motion of the sprites using several types of commands. Firstly, we saw how absolute motion control work, then we had the opportunity to learn more about relative motion commands that allow you to move sprites concerning their direction or position. There were a lot of examples in which you could practice how to draw using the pen commands and experiment with different blocks such as the repeat block that helps you create longer and more complicated codes. Additionally, we discussed some more advanced shapes and patterns that you can use for your programming improvement. In the end, we guided you through the creation of two complete applications while discussing a new topic- Scratch's "create clone" block. The next chapter will be dedicated to some other engaging features of this programming language.

Chapter 3

Looks and Sounds Palette in Scratch

In this chapter, you will have the opportunity to learn more about commands that can be found in the looks and sound categories. Also, like in every other chapter, you will have a lot of practical examples that will allow you to create new projects in Scratch. After you go through every topic of this part of the guide you will be able to use image effects and create your own animation; you will understand how layers operate in Scratch; you will know how to compose music and play sound files in Scratch and last but not the least, we will guide you through another set of complete applications, this time we will use animations rather than games. When you enter the looks palette you will see the commands that will allow you to create graphic effects such as fisheye, whirl, etc and later apply those graphics to either costumes or backgrounds of your projects. Additionally, sound palette enables you to add preferred voices, sounds or music to any application that you want to make. Some of the commands from both palettes you already used in your previous projects.

The Looks Palette in Scratch

As you know, pen commands allow you to draw images directly to the stage panel. However, costumes can be a much more powerful asset for your project and it is an easier way to add desired graphics to your application or animation. This is where the looks palette comes in. It allows you to manipulate the costumes of your sprites to make animations. You can add various effects, create speaking or thinking bubbles or you can change the visibility of the sprite. In this section, we will explore some of the most frequently used commands in this category.

How to make an animated costume

Until now, you learned how to move one or multiple sprites from one point to another on the stage panel. Still, having static sprites isn't always the best solution and sometimes it will be more effective if you can make them move around. You can change that and use several different costumes, then switch them really fast. This way it will look like the sprites in your project are moving. You can test this feature by opening the file named animation.sb2.

This application file has one sprite with seven different costumes attached to one script. When you start running the application all seven costumes will appear in the costumes tab and seven following scripts can be found in the scripts area of the sprite. By clicking the green flag, you activate the application which means that the figure (in this case stick-shaped one) will appear on the stage panel and it will look like its walking. The reason why this stick sprite looks like that is the set of commands for every costume. It also instructs the sprite to put all of the costumes on the list, change them fast and roll over to the first costume from the list. Once you click the green flag, the activated script uses the forever block for the loop and wait for a block for delay after each costume change. This delay is usually set to be 0.1 seconds. If you want to make your sprite run, just remove this delay and the costumes will change instantly which will produce the effect of running. You can take your time and experiment a bit with values for the wait block along with the one that commands costumes to move. Observe how these changes affect the animation of the sprite and choose the one that you like the most. Although drawing a stick isn't complicated and you could have done it without using the costumes tab and looks palette, the code that you would need for the same effect would require much more effort and it would be longer. Contrarily, when you use costumes, the programming of their animation isn't that hard.

If you want to make your sprite more interactive, you can do that by changing its costume so it can respond to a click of the mouse. We will take the example of the "Click on face" application that you can find on the internet. In Scratch, this application has just one sprite named "face", and it has five costumes that are connected to that sprite. This sprite is coded to use "when this sprite clicked" block that can be found on the events palette and it instructs the sprite when it should change the following costume. When you start this application, every click of the mouse on the image changes the face. Generally speaking, it is a command to switch the image from one to another and the mouse click triggers it. This script has one additional function, which uses backdrops' "to" block that instructs the stage panel to switch to one of its four backgrounds randomly. When the stage panel comes to its fourth image, the face-shaped sprite uses the backdrop's "switches to trigger" block (also from the events category) and detects this situation. In that case, the face sprite travels from the upper part of the stage to the center of the panel.

You can try out using some other applications. For example, you can open the file named trafficlight.sb2, which also has one sprite in the shape of the traffic light, as its name suggests. But this time there are three costumes connected to the sprite and they correspond with the green, orange, and red colors. Since this file has an incomplete script you can try to implement the same principle from above and make the traffic light work.

Keep in mind that you can change scenes or levels of your animation by using the "switch backdrop" command. Remember that all sprites in the project can use block such as "use when the backdrop switches" to recognize when the stage panel changed the background, thus change the sprite's costume along with it. If you need more details, you can always open the Tips window that is located on the Scratch web interface.

Creating Sprites That Think or Speak

If you want to make sprites look even more entertaining you can make them think and speak like characters in the comic books. This can be achieved simply by selecting commands named the same way, and you can type in any phrase that you want into white areas of these two commands. After you finish your command, a message will be displayed in a bubble above the sprite instantly; and if you want to clear the text just use these blocks with empty text areas. There is an option that allows you to set a message that will be displayed only for a certain amount of time. For example, you can command the sprite to execute the say block for 10 seconds or think block for two, and so on. If you want to try out a simple simulation first you can open argue.sb2 file and run it. This application shows a fight between two characters in Scratch and you can use the scripts and try to make a similar kind of animated conversation.

Image Effects in Scratch

If you want to add different graphic effects to your sprites you can do that by using the set effect block that will enable you to apply different backdrops and costumes. We already mentioned some of these effects, and in Scratch, they have names like a ghost, mosaic, whirl, fisheye and so forth.

Now, if you want to apply a certain effect you need to click the down arrow first. Then you have to use the "set effect to" block to chose the one that you want from the drop menu. Also, you can use "change effect by" block to adjust the desired effect, which means that you don't have to set it directly. For instance, if you choose the ghost effect which has a current setting to 40, changing it by 60 would make it disappears from the stage panel (just like ghosts are supposed to do) and when you want to change an image to its original setting you have to activate the "clear graphic effects" block to do so. Note that you are not limited to use only one effect at the time, you can set many effects to one sprite. However, this means that you will have to use multiple commands in one graphic effect sequence.

Size and Visibility of the Sprites

It is not a rare case that you need to have sprites of different sizes and appearances when you are making a program. For example, you may want some sprites to look closer than the others, which means that they have to be larger. Or, in another case scenario, you can just use sprites as instructions at the beginning of the program. Changing the size of the sprit is simple and straightforward. You go to the "set the size to %" block and just put the number that you need. The first value that is set to this block is the original size of the sprite while entering another number means that you will modify the size to your preference. If you want to make the sprite look more or less visible, you will have to use hide block or show block accordingly.

For instance, open the file named sneezingcat.sb2 and run the application. You will see all of these commands in action presented with a sneezing cat, as its name suggests. This cat changes its size while sneezing like in cartoons, which means that the size of the cat-shaped sprite grows while the cat is preparing to sneeze and after its sneezes, it goes back to its previous size. You can try and add a more dramatic effect on the sneezing by making the cat disappear afterward. The simplest way to do that is to add a block to the end of the script.

Layers in Scratch

Looks palette has two more commands. These commands affect the order of sprites and the way that they will appear on the stage. This order determines the priorities of sprite visibility if they overlap. Let's say that you want to make a scene in which a boy stands behind a tree. There are two ways to layer this image. If you want the boy to be behind the tree, you must bring the tree to the front layer or send the boy to the back layer. In Scratch, you have two options that allow you to change the order of the layers. These are: go back and go to front commands (layers). The go-to front command tells the program to always put the desired sprite on the top while the other sprite ends up at the back for as many layers as you want. You can try out running the layers.sb2 file, which has four sprites that move through the stage panel. You can change the position of these sprites by pressing the first letter of its color on the keyboard.

The next section is dedicated to the sound palette that can liven up your animations and make them more entertaining.

The Sound Palette in Scratch

Most of the applications that you will create (especially games) require sounds to point out the different moods or background music that will add the emotion you want. In the following text, you will learn more about blocks in the sound palette and how to incorporate them while using audio files and playbacks. Then we will go through some of the commands that are used for playing instruments such as drums and how to change music's tempo and notes that you want to play.

Playing Audio Files in Scratch

As you already know, computers support many formats of audio files. However, Scratch supports only two: MP3 and WAV. You have three kinds of command block that you can use to add sound to your project. These commands are: play sounds until done block, play sound block and stop all sounds block. The first two commands play sounds that you imported with one difference: the play sound block lets the next command until the sound finishes, but the play sound until done block doesn't allow other commands until the selected sound finishes. If you use to stop all sounds block, it will instantly turn off all sounds in the project. The easiest way to add background music is to use one audio file and then play sound until done which will allow the entire file to play and then restart until the application stops running.

Sometimes there can be short breaks after two restarts, it depends on the audio file if they are going to be noticeable or not. If you want to have more control over the play duration you can use the play sound block combined with the wait block. You can experiment with the waiting time and try to produce a smooth transition between the playbacks.

Playing Drums in Scratch (Other Sounds included)

When you start developing games you will often want to use short sound effects. These effects can be the sign of hitting the target for example or finishing a level and so forth. The easiest way to create these sounds is to use "play the drum for beats" block that has 18 drum sounds from which you can choose the one that you like. Each of these sounds has a certain number of beats, and you can add pauses between by applying the "rest for beats" block. If you want to see these commands in action, the best way is to download the beatsdemo.sb2 file and see the effect that beats parameter has in it. The script of this file has three repetitive blocks with counts of two, four and eight and each block uses the same sound but a different number of the beats.

Let's say that the time axis represents two intervals of 0.2 unit value. This means that the first loop plays drum sounds that are 0.8 units of time apart, which means that there will be two drum sounds in this one. The second loop has four drum sounds, which mean that the pause is 0.4 units apart and so on. Every loop has the same amount of time to complete the action it just has a different number of hits in the same interval. We use the expression "units of time" rather than seconds because the amount of time needed to finish one loop depends on the tempo that you set. If you use the default tempo which is 60 BPM (beats per minute) it meant that each loop will have 1.6 seconds to play. If you choose to double the tempo, the time for loops to finish changes too and they will now have 0.8 seconds to complete the command. The same principle applies if you slow the tempo, it just increases the number of seconds.

Composing Music in Scratch

Scratch allows you to use other sounds, not only those that can be found in its library. In fact, you can even compose your own songs and set commands that play notes. When you open the sound palette you will find a "play note for beats" block. Click on the block and select one of the 127 notes adding the number of beats that you want.

If you use "set instrument to block" command from the same palette it will tell Scratch what kind of instrument you want to have to play the selected note. These two commands enable you to create a whole song if you want.

Control of the Sound Volume

Sometimes, when you have different things happening at the stage panel, you want to use sounds that have a fade-out effect as a response to the situation. For example, if you want to make the airplane fly, you could put the louder sound when it takes off and then the more quite version once that the plane is in the sky and moves farther. Scratch offers blocks that can control loudness or, generally speaking, a volume that you can apply to all drum sounds, musical notes or other audio files that you want to use in your project. Go to the sound palette and find the "set volume to %" block. You can adjust the loudness of the sound by entering the number that you need at that moment. Still, keep in mind that this command refers only to the sprite that is connected to (in some cases it can be connected to the stage too). So if your goal is to play multiple sounds at the same time, and you want all of them to have different volumes, you will have to use the same amount of sprites. If you use "change volume by" command you can increase or reduce the loudness by entering positive or negative numeric values. Negative numbers mean that the sound will be softer, and logically, positive numbers will make the sounds louder. If you want to have the sprite's volume visible on the stage all the time, you can just click the box that appears next to the volume command. You can use these commands for different purposes; you can change them when a sprite hits the target (like in the Pong game that you created in chapter 1) or simulating an orchestra if you put enough effort to make more instruments play simultaneously.

Try opening the volumedemo.sb2 file and start the application. You will see a simulation of a cat that walks into the forest. This file has scripts that use change volume blocks, which make sounds of the cat fade away as it goes deeper into the forest. You can use this script and try making something similar.

Setting the Tempo in Scratch

The last three commands that you will find in the sound palette refer to the speed or tempo that you want the notes or drums to be played for each sprite. As we already mentioned above, the tempo is measured in BTM-s or beats per minute and it works like this: if you set higher BPM-s it means that the notes will play faster, thus the tempo is faster and vice versa. You can choose the tempo you want and slow it down or speed it up, depending on your own preference. If you want to have a constant view of the sprite's tempo on the stage panel you simply check the box that appears next to the tempo command. You can try running the tempodemo.sb2 application and see what kind of tempo is set in it. You can then try to change the tempo and see how the program will react.

Creating complete Scratch projects incorporating commands from Sounds and Looks palettes

Now that you learned how to use the commands in these two palettes, you can add even better effects to all of your next projects. In the following section, we will try to incorporate not only things that we learned in this chapter, but everything that we learned about Scratch in general. The projects that we will try to create are one complete animation of a woman dancing and a complete animation of fireworks. You will see that even though this sounds more complicated, it actually helps you review some of the new blocks and to remember the old ones.

First animation- a woman dancing on the stage

The goal here is to animate a female dancer sprite on the stage panel. The complete script can be found as a danceonstage.sb2 file that you can open in the web interface of Scratch. You are supposed to build the whole scene following the next instructions.

The first step is to start a new Scratch project. If Scratch wasn't running before this, a new project will open automatically once that you start the program. If, however, you already have Scratch running, you need to go to the File menu and select a new project. As always, the new project has a default cat-shaped sprite inside.

The next step is to select the backdrop for your animation. In this case, we will go with the party room that can be found in the indoors category. Delete the default white background and insert the party one since you won't need the one you removed.

If you look carefully at the board and ball sprites you will see that they look like the part of the backdrop. The next thing you will notice is that these sprites are actually created from that backdrop image and positioned so they can cover the sections they are created from. This way you have two additional sprites that can change color, thus making the stage panel for your female dancer more realistic.

The next thing you'll need for this animation is background music. In this project, you should go with the medieval1 file that you can find in the music loop category and import it to the stage while deleting the "pop" sound that appears as default. The following phase consists of adding the script that commands the sound to play along setting the wait time that allows the audio file to restart as smooth as possible. We can say that this time should be 9.5 seconds for this concrete animation. To test if everything works so far click the green flag as usual. If everything is done correctly the audio will repeat continuously and you can stop the script once that you are ready to continue.

Now you need to add the dancer. To do that, you need to replace the cat sprite with the female dancing one. Import dan-a and dan-b costumes that you can find in the people category and don't forget to rename the sprite name from cat to dancer. Now you need to add a script that will move the dancer. Let's say that you instruct the dancer to go 15 steps to the left, change one costume to another and then moves 15 steps to the right, then change the costume again and so on. To make it look like she is really dancing you use the forever block that will make these commands repeat for as long as you want. You can add effects like fisheye to add some variety to the dancer's steps. To check if everything works properly click the green flag and observe the features you added. If you hear background music and see your dancer moving right and left on the stage it means that everything works fine. To make the scene livelier, you can add lights in different colors using the board and the ball sprites that we mentioned before. Additionally, you have spotlight sprites that you can insert too.

If you click the stage thumbnail and select the backdrops tab you will be able to create a ball sprite by right-clicking the thumbnail of the party backdrop that you inserted at the beginning and select the "save to local file" option from the menu that will appear. This action triggers the dialog that enables you to save background image to your local files and you need to know where you saved it because you will have to import it again shortly. After you finish this click on the "upload sprite" button that is located above the sprite list and just imports back the image that you saved a moment ago. This way you have created the sprite that is identical to the one at the backdrop image on the stage panel.

You can name this new sprite simply "ball" and then you can edit its costumes in the paint editor. This time leave only the colorful ball and remove everything else, but don't forget to use transparent color to paint some space around the ball too. When you finish this, place the ball-shaped sprite at the exact location as it was on the backdrop from which you took it so it will look like a part of the image again. Then add the script that will change this sprite's color effect. It should change repeatedly and in continuity so the observer can get the illusion that the small circles on the sprite are changing colors. Board sprite is created the same way as the ball sprite and once that you finish coloring and animating it you just put it back at the same place as before so it can appear to be the part of the image too. Since the dancer and the board overlap, the script is instructed to send the board at the back (2 layers), which means that the dancer is always located at the front. You can do this by selecting the dancer-shaped sprite and using the "go to front" command that can be found at the looks palette. The final sprite that we will add to this animation is the Spotlight. Since there is no script for this sprite, you will need to make one. You need to set the center of the image to be at the tip of the cone-shaped point, which is actually a light beam. The script has to set the ghost effect of the sprite first and make it transparent so it won't influence the backdrop. Then you need to command the sprite to go back one layer, which makes the light beam positioned behind the dancing sprite, thus emanating from the spotlight. Observe your drawing and determine its XY coordinates, make the light beam follow the dancer by using the "point towards" block while changing its color permanently.

When you are done adding this last sprite the animation is completed. Of course, you need to test it a few times, so go ahead and click the green flag to see if your animated party is done. Now, if everything is correct, you should hear the music; see the dancer moving along with the board, ball and spotlight sprites that change color like in real discotheque. The next animation will use different graphic effects that we have been mentioning in this chapter.

Second animation – the fireworks

This animation will have a concept of animated firework scene and it will use most of the features that we discussed in this chapter since most of them are connected to the graphics commands. The idea is to make a firework that fills the sky with sparks of different colors. You have rockets that explode into fireworks at random times. Each of these explosions should produce sparks that will fall and slowly fade out. You can start by opening a new project and opening the fireworks_nocode.sb2 file. As in several previous applications that we've used, this one also has initial setup but doesn't have any scripts, which means that you'll have to make them. Firstly, you can conclude that you will need two sprites – one sprite that will represent the city and the other sprite that will represent the rocket for fireworks. The city sprite contains an image of buildings and you can use animations that you like to make it more interesting.

On the other hand, rocket sprite will use the clone feature to create many clones that should explode and produce fireworks. In this phase, you will see that the rocket from the running application has eight different costumes. The first costume is labeled as C1 and it is actually one dot that will be launched to the sky. Once that the dot reaches the destination that is randomly selected it will change to another costume (this change should also be random). This way you will get the effect of an explosion. By using different graphic effects you can make this look even more realistic. Once you finish this, try adding the script to the rocket-shaped sprite and run it by clicking the green flag. When you hide the rocket sprite the forever loop command is triggered and it starts creating clones at randomly picked times. Since we learned that the clones have the same characteristic of the original sprite, all of these clones won't be visible at first which means that you need to add the script that will tell the cloned rocket-shaped sprites what to do next.

These clones should start by using their first costume (the dot) and then move along the horizontal position, which is located at the bottom of the stage panel. Afterward, they should appear on the stage and glide to a random position at some of the upper parts of the grid (in this case that should be above the buildings from the city sprite). The goal of these clones is to make a realistic simulation of the firework's launch and when you run it, it should appear as a red dot that goes towards the sky and when it reaches its final point it simulates an explosion. This explosion is set by using another set of commands that are actually the second part of the script. It consists of clones that play a short sound that resembles the sound of an explosion and the actual explosion. This part starts with the small dot that expands which means that the initial costume with the size set to let's say 20% changes and it enters the loop that increases the size of the explosion and when the loop is finished the current costume deletes itself and another one starts, and so on. When you finish adding this part, the firework animation is complete. Use the green flag to run the complete animation a few times and check everything. We can say that with these two animations you advanced in making a relatively complex program.

Chapter 4

Procedures in Scratch

In this chapter, we will talk about writing separate procedures and putting them together rather than building large and complicated programs as one piece. Procedures make it easier to write codes, thus to test and debug them if needed. Exploring procedures will show you how to coordinate the behavior of multiple sprites by using the message broadcasting; to implement procedures by using the message broadcasting; it will show you how to use Scratch's feature named "build your own block"; and finally, you will learn how to use structured techniques in programming. Most of the projects that you've seen and developed with this guide so far had one sprite. However, applications usually require more sprites that will work together. If we make an animated story as an example, you will see that you need at least a few characters and several different backgrounds. You also need to know how to synchronize the jobs that you assign to certain sprites. This is why we will use this chapter to talk about the message broadcasting in Scratch. It is a mechanism that is used to coordinate the jobs of many different sprites. Then we will see how you can use "custom blocks" command and structure longer programs to become smaller, thus manageable parts that are also known as procedures.

We will use the definition, which says that "a procedure is a sequence of commands that performs a specific function". For instance, you can make a procedure that will instruct sprites to do complex calculations, draw different shapes, process various inputs from the user, play or sequence different notes and many other functions. Once that you create a procedure, you can use it as a building block for some other applications that you want to develop.

Receiving and Broadcasting a Message in Scratch

One of the things that we will determine in this section is how Scratch's broadcast system works in practice. It is not that complicated; every sprite in Scratch can broadcast a message if you use either "broadcast block" or "broadcast and wait for block" that can be found in events palette. These commands trigger every script in every sprite including its own. They begin to work when they receive "I receive" block that is actually a trigger command. This way all sprites in the project "hear" the broadcast but they only act if they have this "I receive" corresponding block.

Let's say that we have four sprites. The first one is a cat, the second one is the frog, the third one is a starfish and the fourth one is a bat. The cat sprite broadcasts "jump" message sending this broadcast to all available sprites including the cat itself. As a response to this instruction, we will take that only the cat and the starfish respond and they jump. The other two sprites didn't continue executing other commands because they didn't have a corresponding block that tells them to obey the broadcast even though they received the message. On the other hand, the "broadcast and wait" block works one the same principle but with one main difference- the broadcast waits until every sprite that received the message finish responding to "when I receive" block before they continue.

Receiving and Sending Broadcasts in Scratch

To show you how sending and receiving messages in Scratch works in practice, we will try to create a simple program that will randomly draw squares in color. The idea is that when the uses the left button of the mouse on the stage panel, the panel detects it and uses the "when this sprite is clicked" command to broadcast a square message (we will call it square in this example but you can use any name you like). When all the sprites receive the message (in this case it is just one sprite) it will use the current position of the mouse and draw a square at that point.

These are the steps that you need to follow to make this application:

Firstly, you need to start Scratch, go to the File menu and select a new project so you can start a new application. The cat costume that appears by default can be replaced with any costume that you want.

Secondly, you have to add "when I receive" command that can be found on the events palette to the scripts area of the sprite that appears on the stage panel. Then you select a new message from the drop menu that appears when you click the down arrow. Once that the dialog box appears, type "square" and press OK. See if the name of the block changed into "when I receive square", if the name has changed into this one, you can proceed.

The third step is to complete the script by lifting the sprite's pen and moving it to the current position of the mouse. This position should be indicated by XY blocks that can be found in the sensing palette. Then you should pick a pen color, lower it, and draw the square.

If everything is done correctly, the sprite should be able to execute the message once it receives it. We can call this script a message handler because, as its name suggests, its job is to make sure that the sprite can process the message.

The final step is to add the code in the stage panel that will broadcast the message that instructs "square" as a response to the mouse click. The easiest way to do this is to click on the sprite list, choose the stage, and add two scripts to it. The first one should clear all pen traces from the stage once that the green flag is clicked. On the other hand, the second script is activated when the user clicks on the mouse and uses it to broadcast a message to the sprite that it should draw the square. With this action, the intended application is complete and you can test it. If every mouse click has a response of square drawings on the stage panel it means that you have successfully completed the program.

Coordinating Multiple Sprites by using Message Broadcasting

This section explains how multiple sprites react to the same broadcast message in Scratch. For better understanding, we will also use an application. This time it will be drawing few flower-shaped sprites on the stage panel as a response to the user's click on the mouse. This application will have five sprints that we will name flower1, flower2, flower3, flower4, and flower5. These sprites are responsible for creating (drawing) five flowers on the stage panel assuming that each sprite has its own costume. However, the background of each costume is transparent and the location of the costume's center of rotation should be marked with crossed lines. The goal is to make the sprite react to the message "flower", to draw and then stamp few rotated copies of the costume located on the stage panel. The next thing is to add the script that will respond to the mouse click. When the user clicks the mouse the stage panel should detect it using the "when this sprite clicked" command, and as a response, it should clear everything in its background broadcasting only one message that we will name " draw". All of the five sprites that we mentioned above should respond to that message and execute the script of drawing flowers that will appear on the panel. The script can be adjusted to assign different and random values to some effects such as brightness, color or size, thus change the entire appearance of the flower. Then it should move to a random vertical position and draw and stamp rotated copies of flower-shaped costumes like the sprite before. You can try opening flowers.sb2 file and running it to check how it works. Although this might seem like a simple code, outputs are really interesting. You can experiment with many different flower types, colors, costumes; you can change their center and search for some other designs. Now that we covered how broadcasting works we will introduce you to the way of managing large programs by making structured, smaller programs instead.

Small steps for Creating Large Programs

Even though some scripts that you used so far are more complicated than the others, they were all relatively short, thus simpler. At some point, you will have to write scripts that will contain several hundreds of blocks or even more which is why it is very important to understand how to maintain and understand them better. This can be a challenging process; however, there is an approach that can ease things up. Structured programming is a term introduced in the 1960s. It refers to a process of simplifying the writing and maintaining the computer programs, therefore have a deeper understanding of them. Unlike the previous approaches that were based on writing single large program codes, structured programming is based on the premise that the program should be divided into smaller pieces so that every part of the program can solve a part of its overall task.

There is an interesting example of comparing this process to a cake recipe, which we will use to illustrate this matter. The first principle that is similar to the cake recipe and structural programming is the fact that they both break down a general problem into the smaller, distinct and logical steps. This way you can come up with a solution for your problem and when it comes to programming this means dividing the problem into manageable parts. This kind of approach also helps you to have a clear view of the program's purpose and its relationship with all other parts or components.

Consider that you need to write a long script that has a purpose of drawing shapes on the stage panel. This script can be divided into smaller parts- logical blocks that are categorized by their function. For example, the first five blocks are used to activate the sprite, and then the first repeat block instructs the sprite to draw a square while the second block commands the sprite to draw a triangle and so forth. If you use structured programming, these related blocks can be grouped together and use one name that will represent them and this way the related blocks become procedures. When you write a procedure you can set them in certain sequences and solve programming issues that are also related.

You can also see how procedures that are separated can be put together and perform the same function as the original script of the program. Of course, the script that uses procedures is modified to be shorter than the original, which makes it more understandable. Using procedures can help you avoid writing the same codes multiple times. With this approach multiplication of the same code is unnecessary. Also, instead of writing commands for many places in the program so they can to execute an action, you can use a procedure that performs all of the commands you need and just use that procedure instead. This kind of strategy in which you can escape from duplicating the code is also known as the code reuse.

For example, in the application of square drawing that we mentioned before the code was reused.

The procedure allows you to implement the war strategy known as "divide-and-conquer" to solve more complex problems. For instance, you can " divide" problems into sub-problems and "conquer" these sub-problems one by one, finding the solution individually. When all of these smaller problems are resolved, the solutions are put back together so they can solve the original problem that was divided in the first place. If you asked yourself how these procedures are created, we have to tell you that before Scratch 2, that wasn't possible. This version of Scratch, released in 2013 added one very important and powerful feature that changed everything. This feature is known as "custom blocks".

Creating Procedures by using Message Broadcasting

In this section, we will see how procedures can improve the code that was used in the application of flower drawing that we used earlier. Start with opening the file named flowers2.sb2 that has a new version of the program that you will use for this exercise. The stage script is the same as before which means that the stage broadcasts the message, which says " draw" at the moment that the user clicks on its mouse. However, in this version, the application uses one sprite and not five like before. This single sprite that we use now has five different costumes. We can name them leaf1, leaf2, leaf3, leaf4 and leaf five. In this scenario, your task is to call a procedure that will draw a flower for all of the five costumes individually. And because you have only one sprite to use, you will need only one copy of the code for drawing instead of five scripts from the previous application. This way, you avoided the duplication of the code, thus you made the program smaller and more understandable. So when the sprite receives the message " draw" broadcasted by the stage, it executes this one script that we mentioned above. This script sets the position for the drawing and the costume and starts the loop in which each of the five flowers is drawn. Every time the loop passes, the Y coordinate triggers the draw flower procedure and broadcasts a message to itself which stops other script's executions until the procedure is done. When the procedure is finished, the " draw" script continues working and adjusts the coordinates and the costume for the flower to come.

Building Your Own Block in Scratch

As we already mentioned, Scratch 2 introduced a new feature for creating your own commands using custom blocks. The blocks that you make usually appear on the more blocks palette and you can use them like any other block in Scratch. We will use the flower application again and modify it so we can view the use of custom made blocks.

Firstly, you should open the file named flower2.sb2 and select filer4download from the File menu so you can save this file under the name flower3.sb2 or some other name that you like.

The second step is to click at the flower sprite's thumbnail and select it. After that, you should look for more blocks palette and select a " make block" option. Name it drawflower, click OK and the new block or new function will appear under that name in the more block palette and in the script area.

The next phase is to detach the script that is connected to the "when I receive" drawflower command and try to connect it to the functional drawflower block that you've made. The result of this is a new procedure that now has a name drawflower and that you succeeded to incorporate into the script as a custom block. Afterward, you should delete "when I receive" drawflower block that you detached because it doesn't have a purpose anymore.

The last step is to add a handler that will call this procedure that you created from the draw message. You can do that by simply modifying the message handler and replace the broadcast and wait for a block with the new custom block that you've made. When this is done, the application is modified and complete and you can test it. Try to click the mouse anywhere on the stage panel to see if the program works as before.

Passing Parameters to Custom Blocks in Scratch

For a better understanding of this section, we will immediately start creating a custom block that we can name "square" in this example. This square, when drawn, should have sides, which are 100 pixels long.

The procedure for square shape is limited with capabilities because we have a fixed size of the sprite. If you want to draw squares of different sizes you can just make a few custom blocks and enter the desired side lengths. Let's say that the values of these lengths are 40, 65 and 150, name your custom blocks square40, square65 and square150, but keep in mind that creating multiple blocks has some complications. In most cases, whenever you make one change, you have to look for all of the copies and apply the same change to them too. A simpler solution is to have only one square block but adjustable length when calling it, which is a concept that you've already applied more than once.

For instance, in Scratch, you can use a single move command that enables you to determine how many steps the sprite will move in the desired direction. This block has a parameter slot in which you can add a numeric value that you want. This way, you don't need a new block whenever you want to change the distance. If we get back to the current program, we see what we have to do- we need to add a parameter slot to our custom made square block so the user can enter the length of the square's side and change it if needed. To modify the square block you need to go to the " define square" block that is located on the scripts area and selects the edit option from the drop menu. When the edit block dialog appears to click the mall arrow to expand it and check all of the options available. For this particular application, you need an option that will allow the block to accept different numbers that refer to the length of the square sides. This is why you will choose "add number input" option from the drop menu and you will be able to set a number slot to your square block. However, you should only add one named number1. If you want to indicate that the slot has some other purpose now you can change the default "number1" name to let's say "side". It doesn't matter how you'll name it as long as it reflects the function or the meaning of the parameter that you have to set.

With this, you have everything that you need to add a number slot, just click OK and the slot is a part of the procedure, which means that your square block can accept numbers as inputs. Some of the problems that users might face are how to determine what the number that he passed means? In Scratch like in every other program, a numeric value can have several meanings. Still, Scratch designers made sure to avoid this kind of confusion by adding labels to the slots and we will use their idea and do the same thing for the square block. Click at the "add label text" option, type the steps and click OK to confirm. If you want to examine the square procedure and its definition in the scripts area, you should see a block that we named side (the name is added to the header of the block). The move block of the procedure still has a fixed number 100 in it, but now you can change that by dragging the side block from the header of the square procedure and put it over the parameter slot of the move command while changing the number 100 to any other number that you want.

On the other hand, the label side that you can see in the header of the Square procedure is also known as a parameter. Another way to define a parameter is to think of it as of the placeholder. Generally speaking, instead of hard-coding a fixed number inside the procedure we used a parameter that we named the side that allows the user to change the size of the square. The user is the one who determines the parameter. In this case, the number 100 can be seen as an argument and it is passed to the square procedure so when the square is executed the side parameter is originally set to 100. This value replaces all other occurrences that can happen to the side block while the procedure lasts. The ability to determine arguments and use them into procedures is a strong feature that helps programs to be more flexible. If you add another parameter such as the color of the square block it will enhance the project even more.

Arguments vs. Parameters

Even though many people who are professional programmers use terms such as argument or parameter like they are one and the same thing, the fact is that they are different. To explain it better we will say that there is an average procedure that can compute the average of two numbers labeled as num1 and num2, which are the parameters of the procedures at the same time. The number 100 and number 50, in this case, are arguments. As you can see, the parameter determines an input to a procedure, but the values of these parameters are called arguments. Even though the number of parameters and number of arguments has to be the same they are not the same thing.

We can conclude this section with some tips that you can use to deal with custom blocks if necessary.

- You should know that custom made blocks can't be divided among sprites. If you create one custom block for one sprite, only that particular sprite can use that block. Also, if a custom block is defined for the stage panel, the only scripts that can call these blocks to action are those that belong to the stage.

- You should always name your parameters meaningfully; it will help others understand what the block is used for.

- If you want to delete a custom block that you made you can do that by dragging the hat block that is located on the scripts area and dropping it over the palettes. Keep in mind that only defined blocks can be deleted and they can't be connected to any stack of other blocks. This means that if you really want to delete a custom block, you will have to make sure that it is not connected to any script first.

- If you want to delete custom block's parameter just click at the name of the parameter that is located in the edit block dialog and find the x icon that can be seen above the slot.

Nested Procedures in Scratch

We explained earlier that every procedure should perform a single well-defined task. However, executing multiple tasks is both good and desirable, especially if you can make one procedure to call another. Nesting procedures are one of the procedures that can provide this kind of flexibility, which especially useful for structured programming. We will use the same square procedure from previous sections to show how this procedure works too. Still, we will create an additional procedure that you can name "squares" for example. The idea is to use this procedure to make four squares that are stretchered by calling the initial square procedure four times. Furthermore, each call should use a different argument value, which will make outputs different too and, for example, we can get four squares that share the same corner. This nested procedure can be used to make some more artistic creations. The next thing that you can try to make is a procedure that you can name rotatedsquares. Rotatedsquares are the procedure that will call the previous squares procedure a few times and turn the angle of the shapes after every call. In this case, we have two parameters, the first one is the parameter that determines the number of repetitions, and the other one is to calculate the angle that each shape will turn after calling the procedure. You can always experiment using different values that will change the patterns and make even more interesting outputs.

Working with Procedures in Scratch

You have learned why it is important to use the structured approach and divide the programs that you develop into the smaller parts. So the next thing that needs to be discussed is how this division is performed. In programming, there aren't any "one size for everything" solutions because every problem is different. This section explores the process of making modular pieces of the larger programs and explains how this division keeps a logical structure regardless of the number of these modules.

How to break a program into procedures

The main thing that you have to know if you want to solve any programming problem is that you need to fully understand the problem itself. Only if this condition is met you can plan on finding a general solution and dividing the problem into major tasks to make it easier. There aren't any right or wrong ways for the division of any program, and you will need some experience to grasp the real meaning of " major" when it comes to tasks. Still, if you structure your plan from overall issue to its specific problems it means that at least you have the correct logic. This problem-solving strategy can be illustrated with an example too. Let's say that you want to draw a house. Here we have a simple problem and we can focus on finding the best strategy without thinking about some particular details. However, even if it looks like a simple task, there is a problem- too many solutions. Some of the possibilities are:

- You can view the house as drawing simple straight lines, in which case the main task will be to draw each line.

- You can view the house as it was made up of six shapes: two sides, two doors, a triangle that represents the roof and a parallelogram. In this case, drawing each shape represents one major task per shape.

- Additionally, if we suggest that the doors have identical shape we can set that drawing one door is a major task and then invoke that task for the second door.

- We can also assume that the parallelogram and the triangle are one unit of the house – the roof. This means that we can say that instead of drawing these two shapes separately, the main task is to draw the roof.

- There is a possibility of viewing one side of the house and the door on it as one unit too. In that case, drawing this unit would be one of the major tasks rather than drawing the side and the door separately, and so on.

There are many other options but the point is the same- the tasks should be small and understandable so you can solve them and focus on one task at the time.

Building Up with Procedures in Scratch

There is one more way to try solving large problems in programming and it's trying to focus on the smallest details first and then look at the overall solution. The idea here is to start from the bottom and once that you solved all of the existing pieces you assemble them in a way they can provide a rational and correct solution for the general problem. We will use one more procedure to illustrate this problem-solving strategy too. We will keep it simple and assume that you have to draw one leaf so let's name the whole procedure that way. Additionally, let's assume that this procedure has a repeat loop command that will run twice while drawing two halves of that leaf, and the halves are drawn as series (15 segments each), and there is an angle of six degrees between them. Let's say that this procedure is our starting point. Now, you can draw a more complicated shape that has five leaves for example. This means that you will create a new procedure that you can name leaves. The thing is that the solution to this problem is simple: you had to call the first procedure (leaf) and use a repeat loop applying the turn angle that you also had from the first procedure. Now you have two procedures – leaf and leaves and you can make something even more complicated.

The point of these examples is that the problem can be solved; no matter how complicated it is, if you find solutions for smaller pieces of that problem and glue them together. These problem-solving strategies help you advance from short and simpler procedures to longer and more sophisticated and complex ones.

Chapter 5

Variables in Scratch

In this chapter, we will talk about scripts that can remember and read different variables. Using this feature means that you can write a program that can interact with the user and that it can respond to its input. Through the following sections we will cover the types of data that Scratch supports, we will explore the ways of creating variables and manipulating them and last but not the least topic that we will cover is how to write interactive programs that will receive inputs from its users.

All of the scripts that we covered in the previous chapters were important for improving your programming skills in Scratch. However, all of them lacked some of the main elements of applications that are considered to be large-scaled. Complex programs can remember values, and more advanced ones can even make decisions to perform an action if certain conditions are met. In this last chapter, we will cover the first key element- variables.

We have mentioned many times that in Scratch, scripts can manipulate and process all kinds of data. These data can be classified as inputs and outputs. Additionally, we can say that data is everything that users put into the program (values, responses, etc.) Still, when you try to create more complicated applications, data often needs to be stored or modified; otherwise, it can't perform all of the tasks. In Scratch, data management is done by using lists and variables. This means that in this chapter we will cover types of data in Scratch and different variables and several ways to use them while programming.

Types of data in Scratch

Computer programs usually manipulate many different data to execute commands or provide useful information. These data can include texts, images, numbers, and many others, and since this is one of the most important tasks to know in programming, you must learn the type of data and operations that Scratch can support. Firstly, the version of Scratch that we cover in this guide has built-in support for three different data types: numbers, strings, and Booleans. Boolean is a type of data that can have only two different values and these values are either false or true. All of these data types can be used to test conditions whether there is only one or more. Once that you determine the result you can set the execution path for your program.

We mentioned in the first chapter that Scratch supports both whole numbers and decimals. Now that we talk about variables more briefly, we can say that Scratch doesn't distinguish between them because they are classified as "numbers" regardless of their value. We would also remind that decimal numbers can be rounded to the nearest whole number and to do that you just need to choose the appropriate block from the operators' category.

"In the Shape"

You have probably noticed that blocks and their parameter slots in Scratch have certain geometric shapes. For instance, if you look at the parameter slot in the " move _ steps" block you will see that it is in a shape of a rectangle and that it has round corners. On the other hand, the "Say hello" block has a shape of the rectangle but with the sharp corners. The reason for this is the fact that the shape of the parameter slot depends on the type of data that it accepts. For example, if you try to enter letters into the parameter slot of " move _steps" block, you will see that the Scratch won't allow it and that it will only accept numeric values. When you observe the shapes of parameter slots and function blocks you will see that the slots have three different shapes (two kinds of a rectangle that we already mentioned and additionally hexagon) while the blocks have only two shapes- rounded rectangle and hexagon. Every shape is connected to a certain data type except the rounded rectangle that can accept numbers and strings in some cases. Contrarily the rest of the shapes have particular compatibilities which means that for example, the hexagon-shaped slot will only take the function of the same shape and the other way around. To avoid confusion, Scratch designed a system that prevents the user from mismatching data types. This makes things easier because you don't have to memorize the compatibility of the shapes and data types if you make a mistake, Scratch just won't allow you to proceed because the data types aren't compatible.

Automatic Conversion of Data Types in Scratch

As we already mentioned, the function block that is in the shape of a rounded rectangle can only accept the parameter slot of the same shape. All of the function blocks with this shape that we used so far supported numbers as only data types. This means that as long as we use them to enter a numeric value (number of steps for example) we won't have a problem.

Still, some function blocks have round-rectangle shape and they can support one additional format- strings. These function blocks can be found either on the sensing palette or on the operator's palette. The question is: what will happen if we insert a string instead of a number into parameters slot?

Scratch is designed to try to automatically convert data types if needed. Let's say that the user entered a number 120 in response to the "enter number" command. This input is saved and once that is passed to the "say" block Scratch automatically converts it to a string.

Understanding all types of data that Scratch uses and operations that can perform are really important for further improvement, especially if you are interested in writing more complicated applications. It will help you to comprehend how everything works and why it works that way. The next sections are dedicated to variables and the ways you can store them or use them in your projects.

Variables -introduction

We will start this introduction directly with an example. We will take the well-known game Whack-a-Mole and imagine that we are trying to create software that will make it work. The original concept of the game is smacking the moles with a mallet as they pop out of the holes on the ground. So you have the surface of the ground with holes, a mallet, and moles. However, the version that we will use here is slightly different. We will assume that the player has to click on the sprite that appears at the random locations on the stage panel. The sprite needs to remain visible shortly and then disappear only to reappear again at a different location. The goal of the game is to click on the sprite before it disappears and every successful click means that you scored one point. Now that you have some basic programming knowledge, the question is, how will you keep track of the score that a player achieves? The answer is obvious- you'll use variables. This section is dedicated to variables, which are one of the key elements of every programming language. We will explore the ways of creating variables in scratch and how they can store different data types.

Definition of the Variables

A variable is defined as a "named area of computer memory". We can say that variables are something like data boxes that contain different data types such as text and numbers and that the program can assess all of those data whenever it needs.

For instance, we can pick one variable, we will name it "side" and assume that its current value is 60. Keep in mind that every time you create a variable, a program provides memory so the value and the name of the variable that is stored and allocates it. Once you create a variable you can use the name that you gave her to refer to the particular value that it represents. Let's say that we have a box (or a variable in this case). This box has a name- we will use "side" since we already named the variable, and that box contains a number 60. With this box, we can construct different commands. One of these commands can be to move 4*to the side. When we activate this command, Scratch will find the box named "side" in its memory, it will access its content (number 60) and use the acquired content to replace the label inside the "move _steps" block. The result of executing this command is a sprite that moved 60x4, which is 240 steps.

If we take Whack-a-Mola game as an example, you can use variable to determine the player's score. To do that, you should save a certain amount of space in the Scratch's memory and store the score, and don't forget that it is important to add a functional name to the variable- in this case that would be "score". This way program will always know where to find and change the content inside if needed. At the beginning of the game, you should use the "set score to 0" command to make Scratch look for the variable and put 0 value to it. The next step is to instruct Scratch to "increase sore by 1" so every time that the player catches the sprite, the value of the variable changes and it is stored until it changes again. This change in values is the simplest way to describe or define the variable.

Variables are very important when it comes to the evaluation of algebraic expressions and storing its intermediary results. This function of variables is very similar to the thing we know as dong " mental math". For example, let's say that you have to calculate the result of 3+4+5+7. The easiest thing to do is add 3+4 first, memorize that the result is 7 then add the next number, memorize the result again and so on until you get to the final result. To show the principle in which variables work we will try to write a program that will use the temporary memory storage while computing the expression: (1/5) + (5/7) / (7/8) –(2/3).

There is one more way to write this program. You can use numerator and denominator and evaluate them individually, then use the "say" command and display the result of the division. Or you can calculate the result using two different variables that you'll name num and den in which num stands for the numerator and den stands for the denominator.

Now you can see the arrangement of these variables in Scratch's memory. The num variable looks like a tag that refers to the result of calculating the first part of the expression, thus (1 / 5 + 5 / 7), which is stored. The same way, den represents a variable that refers to the result of calculating the other part of the expression (7 / 8 – 2 / 3) while storing it to Scratch's memory. When you trigger the "say" command, Scratch goes to the content of its memory that is marked as num and then and divides these two values. The final result is displayed on the screen.

This mathematical expression could be broken into even more fractions; therefore, it could use more variables and still show the same result. In the case that we use more fractions to calculate this expression we can say that now we have 4 variables that we will name a, b, c and d. All of these variables hold one certain fraction of the expression. Keep in mind that program will always give the same results but different paths are followed.

This simple math task demonstrated once again that regardless of the complexity there can always be more than one solution to the problem. It can happen that you have concerns about your program's size or speed, or you can just think that its readability is not as good as it should be. Still, this guide has an introductory purpose so all of the scripts and the content have to be adjusted accordingly. Now that we discussed why variables are useful let's move on to the next section.

Using and Creating Variables in Scratch

We mentioned several times the importance of variables in every program. Now, we will talk about them briefly using a simple application attempt that should simulate rolling dices and displaying their sum.

The dice simulator that we will use in this example has three different sprites the player and two dices. We will name the sprites "player", "die1" and "die2" for better understanding. The role of the player is to manage the simulation. When you press the green flag the player sprite should generate two numbers between one and six and save these variables naming them "rand1" and "rand2" for example. The next step is broadcasting a message to the remaining two sprites – two dices (die1 and die2) that are supposed to show values that are randomly generated. As you may suggest, the first dice die1 will always show random values of rand1 while the die2 will always show the values of the second variable rand2.

The next phase is adding the rand 1 and rand 2 to the players sprite and displaying their sum using the "say" command.

If you want to make the application from the beginning open a new project in Scratch tan opens the file named dicesimulator_nocode.sb2. The file that you added doesn't have scripts but it has the background image for the stage panel along with all of the three sprites that you need in this simulation. We will now create scripts that you need. Firstly find the player sprite, click on its thumbnail and select it. Go to the data palette and locate " make a variable" option. The dialog will appear after the selected option so you have to enter the variable's name and determine its scope. The scope of a variable defines which sprites can execute "write to" or "change value off" commands towards the variable. In this case, enter rand1 as the name of the first variable and select option "for all sprites" for the scope; when you finish click OK to confirm.

Once you create a variable, the data palette will offer you a few new blocks that didn't appear before. These blocks can be used to change the value by a fixed amount or set it to a specific value, they can also be used to hide or show the variable's monitor on the stage panel. To create the second variable you have to repeat the procedure and name it rand2. With this, you should have another variable block that is located at the data palette. Pressing down arrows will let you choose between the first and the second variable. Now that we have these two codes, we have to create the script for the third –player sprite. The first block in this script should instruct the rand1 variable to show a randomly picked number between number one and number six. We will go back to the box analogy; the player's command tells the sprite to go to the rand1 labeled box and place the number that is randomly generated inside it. Another command tells the second variable-rand2 to do the same thing and put a random value between one and six. The next thing is broadcast of the player's message named "roll" to the other sprites die1 and die2 to let them now that they need to switch to the costume that rand1 and rand2 specified. When the sprites finish their job the script continues and the sum of numbers that dices showed appears on the screen using the "say" block.

The next part of the script that you'll need to make for this game simulation is the "roll" message that is broadcasted by the handler.

After you finished with all of the previous scripts, you should drag the variable block named rand1 from the data category and set it to the parameter slot of the switch costumes command to make the script completed. This script contains the repeat command that changes the dice costumes randomly several times so the viewer can get the illusion that the dice is rolling. The number of times that the costume will change can be edited and it will speed up or slow down the imaginary rotation depending on the number you want. The next thing is the costume number that is specified by the rand1 variable.

Keep in mind that dices should have six costumes each and that they should correspond to the numbers between one and six. So, if rand1 shows number 4 the costume command should display the costume with four dots on it. The script for the second dice or die2 is almost identical as for the first dice. And since the second dice is supposed to respond to the second variable, the easiest way to set up the code is to duplicate it from the first dice and just replace rand 1 with rand2 on the second dice. With this, you have completed the dice simulator and you can test the completed version again by clicking on the green flag and observing the simulation in action to make sure that everything functions.

Variables and their scopes

There is one more concept related to variables that you should pay attention to. As we mentioned before, the scope establishes which sprites can change the value of that variable or write to that variable. The scope of the variable can be specified and you can create it by selecting a certain option. In the first case, you can choose the "for this sprite only" option, which will create variables that can only be changed by the sprite that owns them. In this case, all other sprites can use and read the value of that variable but they can't write to it.

Let's say that the classic Scratch's sprite – the cat has a variable. We will name this variable count and we will assume that the scope of the variable is "for this sprite only". If we add another sprite, penguin-shaped for example, it can read the count variable with its X positioned block and using the sensing palette. Once that you set the cat sprite to become the second parameter of this block, the first parameter will allow you to decide what attribute your cat-shaped sprite should have, including its variables.

Still, Scratch doesn't have a block that will allow the other (penguin) sprite to make any changes to the count variable that we placed at the beginning. This means that the penguin sprite can't influence the count; therefore it can't cause any effect that you wouldn't want, especially when it comes to scripts that are running behind the cat sprite. Using "for this sprite only" scope is good for practice especially since they can only be updated if the sprite that has this command does something. These kinds of variables are also known as local variables. The advantage of the local variables is the fact that many sprites can use the same name for naming them without any conflict. For example, if you want to make a racing game, you will have two initial sprites. Both of these sprites can have their local variable that sets the car's motion speed on the stage panel for example. This means that each sprite can change the variable of their speed independently. If you set the speed of one car to be 15 and the second sprite's speed is set on 20 for instance, the second car will move a bit faster.

Variables with the scope that are set "for all sprites", however, can be used, read and modified by any sprite that appears in the project. These kinds of variables are called the global variables, and they are especially useful for communication and synchronization between the sprites. Let's say that you are making a game that has three buttons and every button represents a game level. You can create a global variable and name it "global-level" and set each button-shaped sprite to have this variable with a certain value when clicked. This way it is easy for you to see which levels users preferred. Once that you set "for all sprites" scope the cloud checkbox of the variable becomes available. It is a feature that enables you to store variables on Scratch's server otherwise known as the cloud.

Blocks that are connected to this server's variables have little squares at their front so you can make a distinction between them and all other variables. If you have variables stored on the cloud, or projects that you shared, anyone who views the projects will be able to see all of the variables of the project. So for example, if you share a game application, cloud variables can be used to track the highest and the lowest scores among the players. These variables update instantly for all those who are interacting with the application and since they are on the Scratch's server, they will remain there even if you exit the program. The most common usage of cloud variables is creating surveys and other similar projects that need to store large numbers over a specified period.

Changing Variables in Scratch

Two command blocks enable you to modify variables. There is a "set to" command that assigns a new value directly to the variable without considering its content at the time. The "change by" is the other command and it is used to alter the value of a variable about its value at the tie, which means that there is a specified amount that can be used for its modification. You can use many different ways to change the variable and still get the same outcome. Let's take three scripts to demonstrate this.

All of these scripts start by setting values for two values. We will name these variables sum and delta and add them 0 and 5 as values. Now, the first script will use the change block and alter the value of the sum by the delta value. The second script will use "set command to" to add the value of the sum to the value of delta and the third script has the same outcome using the temporary variable. Then it adds the sum value to the delta value, saves the results in the "temp" variable and finally copies that value into the value of the sum. When you execute any of these three scripts, each sum will have number 5 in it which makes all three scripts equivalent. Keep in mind that the method used in the second script represents classic practice in programming so you can take more time and explore it more until you become comfortable using it on some other examples too.

Variables in Clones

Each sprite has its associated properties presented in a list. Some of those properties are its XY position, the direction of the sprite and so forth. These lists are actually the current values of each sprite's attribute. If you create a variable for the certain sprite and set the scope to "for this sprite only", that variable becomes an attribute of that sprite. When the sprite is cloned, its clone inherits all of the original sprite's attributes, including the variables.

The value and the characteristics of the variable are identical to the value of the master sprite at the time that the clone was made. Still, attributes of the clones change over time along with its variables. Those changes don't have any influence on the master sprite though. And the same goes for the other way around, any subsequent change that can happen to the original sprite doesn't have any effects on its clones.

To demonstrate, let's assume that the master sprite owns a variable with a current value of 20. We will name this variable "speed. When you create a clone, it will have the same variable, with the same name and with the same value. You can go and change the value of the master's sprite variable from 20 to 30, but the clone's speed value will remain 20. This concept can help you make a difference between the clones in your project.

For example, we can set the master sprite that has a master variable that we will name cloneID1. When you click the green flag, the loop starts and creates tree clones of the master sprite and sets their names to cloneID2, cloneID3, and cloneID4. Each clone has its own copy of cloneID with different values. Now you should use the block "if" to see if every ID will perform a corresponding action and then test and observe the behavior of the clones when they interact with global variables. As a reminder, we will say once more that the global variables are variables that have their scope set with "for all sprites" block which means that any sprite can read and change them. The same thing applies to the clones.

As an example of this, we will use the script to detect when all of the clones from the master sprite disappear. The script is based on the master sprite that sets the global variable. This variable is named numclones and its value is five, thus it creates five clones. The script waits that the numclones variable becomes zero so it can announce the end of the game. Clones appear at random locations and times saying "hello" for three seconds and then they disappear. Numclones value decreases every tome that the clone is deleted; every deleted clone means one point less than before. When all of the five clones disappear and the numclones value reaches zero the main script doesn't wait anymore and the master sprite declares that the game is over.

Getting Input from Users in Scratch

The best way to demonstrate this feature is to assume that you want to create a game that will allow children to learn about the basics of arithmetic. The game should have sprites that would show a problem to a child and ask to enter the correct answer. The question is how can you use the input of the player and determine if the answer is correct or not? Luckily, Scratch has a sensing palette that has a command block named "ask and wait". You can use this block to read inputs from each player. This block uses one parameter, which shows a string in the form of the question to the user. Still, execution of this command has different outputs, which depend on the visibility of the sprite – it can be hidden or shown. These outputs appear If the "ask and wait" block is called by the script owned by the stage rather than by the concrete sprite. When the command is executed, the script, which called to action waits for the user to press enter or the input box and then stores the input as a part of an answer block. The execution of the command continues until the block command starts.

Naming Variables

Over the last decades, people have always had their own ideas on how to name the variables in different programs. One of the conventions that are actually quite popular is that the name should start with the lowercase letter and use capital letters for every additional word. Some examples are lastName, sideHeigth, schoolRate, and so on.

Unlike other programming languages, Scratch allows you to name variables using numbers, letters or event the white spaces at the beginning. For example, you can use names such as 1234square or side length. However, the most recommended way to name variables in every programming language is to make sure that the names are meaningful and that you can know immediately what is the function of the variable. If you tend to use one-letter names it can be confusing, especially if you have multiple variables to work with. Contrarily, if you use the names that are too long it can make the script more complicated. Keep in mind that the Scratch is case sensitive so if you name your variables Name, nAme or namE, in Scratch these will be three different variables.

Performing Arithmetic Operations

We can demonstrate this by creating a script that will ask the user to input two different numbers. The script computes these numbers and displays the result in the voice bubble, using the usual "say" command. This script uses two different variables. We will name them num1 and num2 and they store the numeric values that the use enters. Let's say that inputs are numbers 5 and 6, the simplest arithmetic operation is to add them and then show the result. You can make scripts that solve complicated mathematical problems as we already discussed at the beginning of the guide.

Conclusion

In this guide, we have had the opportunity to discuss the most important features in Scratch. Since this guide is dedicated to those who are not that knowledgeable but still interested in programming we tried to keep it as simple as possible. However, we wanted to give you as many entertaining projects that you can try to create on your own as we could. It was important to become familiar with Scratch and with the environment in which you are supposed to work. Furthermore, we explained all of the basic commands that Scratch offers and talked you through the different kinds of games and animations so you can use that material for practicing.

In the end, we dedicated a lot of time to variables which are one of the key concepts of programming, and once that this guide becomes less than you want to know you should feel free to use all of the additional files and resources that we mentioned, at least when it comes to the version of the Scratch that we used in this guide

Becoming a programmer means that you will have to invest time and patience, however, Scratch allows you to explore, play and experiment without paying that much attention to codes. Scratch's design made it user-friendly and every person in the world can use it regardless of their computer science knowledge. Keep in mind that we didn't use the most recent version of Scratch but that they all have the same concept, so you will easily find your way around in every Scratch interface that you use.

Scratch is easy when it comes to sharing your work and collaborating with people around the world too. It is highly recommended that you use all of the features that Scratch offers and to connect with others. Although it is not necessary to have a Scratch account you should make one or at least how to make it and how to use backpacks from Scratch and use it for scripts and sprites that you or others created. There are also additional fun options like remixing projects of other people and being able to publish your own creation with the worldwide community of Scratch.

As we said, the Scratch account is not obligatory; however, it is beneficial in many ways. It provides you with options like sharing projects online or communicate directly with other people. The easiest way to get an account is to visit http://scratch.mit.edu/, which is called Scratch's official website. You will find a "Join Scratch" button at the top of the monitor, follow the instructions like adding your name and your password, and when the account is approved- you are ready to go.

When it comes to programming in Scratch, the logged-in members have options of creating a clean project, remixing one or more projects that other people shared on Scratch's website or just use one of the old projects that are there and modify it to its own preference. You can experiment as much as you like which is the most entertaining part. We already mentioned a new project option, so it is really straightforward, you find the "create" option and then the project editor that is built' in Scratch will open. The interface of paint editor for logged and unlogged members is pretty much the same; still, there are few additional options when you are a Scratch's community member! For example, when you are logged in, you can see the backpack panel and two buttons that weren't there before- the first one to see the project page and the other one to share it. Additionally, you will have a username that you chose and a suitcase-shaped icon that will appear at the edge of the toolbar. The File menu will have some new options too.

Another advantage of becoming a member of Scratch's community is that whatever you program using your account, stays automatically saved on the Scratch's server or cloud as we called it before. However, it is still always more useful to click on the "save" option before you close Scratch- just in case.

One of the most entertaining features of the online version of Scratch is being allowed to remix other projects. The idea is simple, just click the button named "remix" and start putting things that you like together. You can always go and click "view the remix tree on the project" to see the progress of your remix and how it evolved since you start editing. And don't worry if other people use your projects in their remixes, once that the finished remixes are shared, the original project creators are always named in Scratch along with the link to the original project.

www.ingramcontent.com/pod-product-compliance
Lightning Source LLC
LaVergne TN
LVHW051743050326
832903LV00029B/2687